I0150477

SECRETS REVEALED

A Journey Into Kingdom Principles

LINDA SANTANGELO

Daniel 2:22 He reveals the deep and secret things…

Daniel 2:22 He reveals the deep and secret things...

ACKNOWLEDGMENTS

I would like to acknowledge and thank some truly significant people in my life who were instrumental in birthing this book, from possibility to reality.

First and foremost, I would like to thank my Heavenly Father, Jesus, and the Holy Spirit, as I couldn't even imagine where I would be today without having met You and starting this wonderful journey. In wanting to write a book of significance that would transform lives, *You* have breathed into the words of these pages and my life.

I also want to thank my husband, Vinnie, who is my staunchest supporter. Without you supporting me, I couldn't do what I do. You believe in me, and your love and faith have spurred me on to become a woman of God with the freedom to follow the call of God on my life. I love you and honor the place you have in my heart!

I am so grateful to both Marios and Danielle Ellinas for all they have poured into my life. I have learned so much from sitting under Marios and his friendship, and for three years in a row, he spoke this book into existence. The first year he spoke it, I didn't believe there was a book within me. The second year he spoke it, I thought possibly. The third year he spoke it again, and the next morning the Lord showed me what the book would be about. I finally knew what he said was right, that I did have a book within me that needed to be written.

But, it wouldn't be until the end of that year that I would begin to write this book. The manuscript was at the publishers another year before it was finally printed. This ended up being a five year process!

Every time I was blocked and thought I couldn't write anymore, the Lord was faithful to give me a little more until it was completed.

I also want to thank Kathy Brooks for your help in editing the portions I rewrote in this revised edition. I value your friendship!

I am grateful to all of you!

SECRETS REVEALED

TABLE OF CONTENTS

WHAT PEOPLE ARE SAYING

"Linda Santangelo is a seasoned believer. In her book, *Secrets Revealed*, she details her amazing journey of walking in the Spirit and the importance of releasing what the Spirit reveals into the earth. This book will both, encourage and challenge you to see behind the scenes, as believers everywhere prepare the way for the great moves of God across the earth. In many ways, Linda's life typifies the life of one of God's great, unsung heroes. Her passion and obedience to advance the Kingdom of God has left an indelible impact in New England. I count it an honor to call her a friend."

Daryl Nicolet
Senior Leader and Founder
Faith Worship Center
Pepperell, Massachusetts
www.faithworship.org

"*Secrets Revealed* is a vulnerable account of the relationship and the revelation that comes through journeying closely with the Father. Jeremiah 29:13 says, "*You will seek me and find me when you seek me with all your heart.*" As Linda candidly shares her experiences and encounters, you will find the desire awakened in you to seek the fullness of His plan for your life. Linda shares keys to discovering the assignment and authority each one of us has been given. *Secrets Revealed* will challenge you to overcome the difficult circumstances of this life through desire, diligence, and commitment. Linda is a passionate friend of God, truly demonstrating a life of faith and authority on this earth. If you desire a more fruitful and deeper walk, you've picked up the right book. Get ready to discover the mysteries of His grace and love in the pages that follow."

Danielle Ellinas
Radiant Destiny International
Old Saybrook, Connecticut
www.radiantdestiny.com

"In a day and age where it seems as though we're on 'slippery slopes' of church culture and personally carrying out His assignment, out comes this book, *Secrets Revealed*. With her finger on the pulse of intriguing truths of God, Linda Santangelo captures with clarity the heart of God partnering with His people. She does this with a beautiful collision of amazing personal experiences and deep insights into how God addresses us individually and corporately to reveal His secrets."

"*Secrets Revealed* takes you deeper into practical applications of dealing with life and church in powerful, healthy, and meaningful ways. You will be impacted and blessed by Linda's ability to write both simple and deep, from both personal experience and revelation of God's Word."

Ron Kutinsky
Senior Leader
Hope International Ministries
Bradenton, Florida
www.moreofhim.org

"Linda Santangelo's book, *Secrets Revealed*, will stir you to dive deeper into your journey with the Lord. With great pleasure, I highly recommend this book. You will receive fresh revelation from Heaven as you read Linda's journey into learning Kingdom principles. I've known Linda for some years, and she has a wonderful anointing to transform lives and regions. This book will help you to see the impossible become possible in day–to–day living. Get ready to receive fresh revelation from the Lord, and get ready to live a supernatural lifestyle!"

Lisa Buldo
Founder of Lisa Buldo International
www.LisaBuldo.com

FOREWORD

It is my strong conviction that the magnitude of inspiration issuing forth from a publication is directly related to the author's stature and character. Linda is a woman of great stature and exceptional character; therefore, *Secrets Revealed* is not only instructive and edifying, it is predominantly inspirational.

With great love and care and with characteristic boldness, Linda challenges us to grow by gleaning from her voyage through life. She welcomes us in and takes us on the journey with her, all while serving as our most insightful tour guide every step of the way.

In a very similar manner to that of her outstanding speaking ministry, Linda teaches with authority – the measure heaven grants to those who understand Kingdom government. She testifies with credibility – the kind people gain as they go through difficulties with the right perspective and attitude. She imparts truth with integrity – the badge God pins on the hearts of those who are wholeheartedly committed to His ways.

Danielle and I consider it a high honor to walk alongside Linda and Vinnie Santangelo. They are a remarkable couple in God's Kingdom. Linda has always been one of the most honorable and loving sister to us. She beautifully models the insatiable hunger to grow in Christ; willingly shares everything she receives from His bounty; tenaciously seeks, finds, and squeezes the glory in every circumstance; and faithfully presses toward the mark of God's high calling in Jesus.

Linda's *Secrets Revealed* is a product of a life well–lived for His glory, and it will undoubtedly be a huge blessing to everyone who partakes of its treasure!

Marios Ellinas
Senior Leader
Valley Shore Assembly of God
Old Saybrook, Connecticut, USA

A Principal of The Nest Online Training Base
Levin, New Zealand

WHAT ARE THE SECRETS BEING REVEALED?

"This secret was hidden throughout the ages and generations, but has now been revealed to His saints, to whom God wanted to make known the glorious riches of this secret."
Colossians 1:26–27 (ISV)

Secrets are stored up in the Word of God for those who seek them out, for those who have a heart to know the purposes of God for their lives and for the earth.

In Matthew 13:45–46, Jesus is telling us the Kingdom of God is like a pearl of great price, where a man sold everything he had in order to purchase it. How many of us are willing to be totally sold out to the Kingdom of God in order to purchase the pearl of great price? To really press into the Kingdom, to learn the secrets held for those willing to pay *any* price to obtain them. These secrets lead to greater authority and destiny being released in our lives. This book will share *many* Kingdom secrets in each chapter to help us be transformed and prepared to carry the weight of His glory into our destiny.

I have learned a lot of secrets during my journey deeper into the Kingdom of God. I learned principles that took me further into the government of God and taught me how to live with true authority in ruling and reigning. Secrets we apply thrust us deeper into greater authority in the Kingdom of God. These secrets always come by paying a great price in yielding to the Word of God. I wouldn't trade any of these secrets, as they have led me to freedom, governmental authority, and destiny.

Secrets are *revelations*, which comes from the word, reveal, meaning to *'lift off the veil'* or *'remove the cover.'*

**Revelation is given for one primary
purpose: personal transformation.**

Encounters with the living Word bring paradigm shifts in our life. First, in our thinking and then in what we experience. Change your thinking, and you will change your life.

**The secret is found in *living* out the Word
of God, not just in knowing it.**

We may think we already know these verses, but the secret is found in living them out. It's about walking where our life is totally, radically transformed; and we are taken much deeper into Kingdom authority. Promotion from the Lord comes to those who are willing to sacrifice everything, like the man in the parable of the pearl of great price, in order to live out the principles contained in this book. For once you do, you are able to teach them to others. Otherwise, you will have no authority to teach principles you have not lived by.

In the process of learning how to walk in governmental authority, I've also learned to value the *caves* in my life, which are those places where character is formed in the difficult tests of life we all walk through while on this earth.

I am praying the *secrets* I've learned in my life, those I share in this book, will help us to be transformed into ever–increase-ing glory.

Personally, it has been quite the journey! Even though there were a lot of difficult lessons to learn, which came from learn-ing many *secrets* in the Word of God, I wouldn't have had it any other way. I paid the price to be released deeper into destiny, and it was worth *everything* I have had to walk through.

> *"Your eyes saw my unformed body; all the days*
> *ordained for me were written in Your book*
> *before one of them came to be."*
> Psalms 139:16

Our destiny is written in heaven in a book with our name on it, and all of our assignments and unique destiny were actually written in our book before we were born. How amazing is that?

Lord, I declare those who read this book will find the secrets for their own life and these secrets will lead them deeper and further into the Kingdom of God. I also declare they will learn how to walk in honor and submission and have great authority.

In Jesus' name, Amen.

SECRET KINGDOM PRINCIPLES

Revelation is given for one primary purpose: personal transformation.

The secret is found in *living* out the Word of God, not just in knowing it.

Chapter 1

WHY DID IT END?

*"And we all, with unveiled face, beholding the glory of the
Lord, are being transformed into the same
from one degree of glory to another. For
this comes from the Lord who is the Spirit."*
2 Corinthians 3:18 (ESV)

I hope you have read the introduction, *'What are the Secrets
Being Revealed?'* before this chapter, as you will have a better
understanding of the secrets shared within these pages.

This book begins with my testimony because this testimony
shaped the very course of my life. It launched me into such a
hunger for the presence of God, in leading me to great transfor-
mations and revelations.

I met the Lord after being married for several years, when
our marriage was in trouble. For nine years after we became

Christians, we went to a denominational church where we received a lot of the Word of God. The church also taught Calvinism, which teaches the Gifts and Baptism of the Spirit are no longer in operation after the apostles died. Salvation was the most important thing in life. Everything including healing was prayed, *"If it be your will....."* Needless to say, we didn't see a whole lot of healing during that season.

Despite that teaching, the Lord broke through with a miracle as we both had fertility problems and couldn't have any children. I read in the bible, about Hannah praying for a son, Samuel, and decided if God would do that for her, then I would also pray for a son. After eleven years of marriage, I became pregnant; and because I prayed exactly like Hannah, I had faith we were going to have a son.

At that time, there was no way to tell the gender of a child, since ultrasounds weren't used until a while later. I would call the baby a *he* and people would caution me it wasn't good to call an unborn child either gender before you really knew what the child would be. I was right as we had a son! Seven months later, I became pregnant with our daughter and eventually, had two more children.

Miracles still happen!

When our firstborn daughter was a year old, something transpired that radically changed the course of our lives. My husband had been having headaches for an entire year but had never been diagnosed. One day, he drove home early from work with a severe headache and didn't wake up the next day. We rushed him to the hospital and found he was in a coma, and dying of a malignant brain tumor. He was also paralyzed on one side of his body, and that same day, I was told he was going to die.

I was overwhelmed by the news; and upon returning home, I cried out to the Lord. I reminded Him how I was not able to conceive for so long, but now had two toddlers and didn't know how I was going to take care of them. Then, I said something to Him that I believed moved His hand. In such sincerity of heart, praying and meaning every word, I spoke a verse from the book of Job:

> *"The Lord giveth and the Lord taketh away;*
> *blessed be the name of the Lord."*
> Job 1:21 (KJV).

The next morning a Spirit–filled friend of mine at the church we attended called and told me I needed to believe he was going to be healed. I replied, "No, as it is up to the Lord and if it is His will, my husband will be healed," as I was really indoctrinated by this teaching. She asked me if I would be willing to receive the faith she had, and I told her, "Yes." She prayed an impartation of faith into me.

At that moment, I was given a gift of faith that I knew, that I knew, that I knew, he was going to be healed. It was a gift because I had no grid to believe for divine healing before that moment.

The next morning at the hospital, the neurosurgeon met me to say the tumor was inoperable, but they could try operating to remove it. He stated that with or without the surgery my husband was going to die. I thought to myself, "Who are you, a mere man, to tell me he is going to die? My trust is in the One who holds the power over life and death!"

The doctor thought I was in shock since I didn't respond the way he thought I should and asked me if I had understood what he had just said. My reply was that I had indeed heard him and also completely understood what he told me.

I told him to operate and also knew that I knew my husband would be made whole. The surgeons removed the tumor and put a shunt in his head because of extreme swelling. After the surgery, the doctor came out and told me because there was so much swelling on his brain, he was going to die in the next few days.

But, I didn't believe what the doctor said!

When he didn't die, I was told he would be paralyzed on one side of his body for the remainder of his life or would not have full function of his brain.

Again, I didn't believe the doctor's report!

Unbeknownst to me, my husband while in that coma, had a heavenly encounter of his own. I didn't find out until much later that he was standing in Heaven before the throne of God, listening to Satan and God arguing over his body and death. We had no grid for this type of encounter! The Lord won that battle and healed him from cancer and death, just as I knew He would!

Because of his heavenly encounter, my husband was transformed into a man of faith and became so excited about everything he saw in the Word of God that I just wasn't able to see. I became extremely frustrated and went before the Lord saying, "Whatever happened to my husband, I want it!"

God kept leading me to the Baptism of the Holy Spirit, but I kept rejecting it because we were taught it was not necessary and Tongues were of the devil. Each time God brought me to this, I would reject it. After the fourth time, I finally realized the Lord kept leading me to this, because it was the truth.

Since my husband had an encounter in heaven and was baptized in the Holy Spirit without asking for it, he didn't understand what had happened to him. When I told him about wanting to ask for it, he cautioned me, as we had been taught for many years. But I was hungering for what I believed was true and went for it. I prayed for the Baptism of the Holy Spirit and felt nothing had happened. So, I asked my husband to pray over me for it and still felt nothing. After reading about all the manifestations of the Spirit in the books I read, and still feeling like nothing happened, I was so discouraged.

The next morning, I read this verse in Matthew 18:19:

> *"Again, truly I tell you that if two of you on earth*
> *agree about anything they ask for, it will be*
> *done for them by My Father in heaven."*

God asked me, "Did two of you agree for the Baptism of the Spirit?" I answered affirmatively. He said, "Then what does it say happened?" I answered, "It says I have it," and He said, "Then just believe it." So, I did ... and was!

We ended up leaving that church and went to another denominational church, as we didn't know any other type. We started a home group that met in our living room with another couple from our old church who had also been baptized in the Spirit

The four of us would worship together with a guitar and contemporary music, just sitting there, telling the Lord, "We will sit here and just wait until you show up." That went on for some time and one night, He did show up and nothing was ever the same!

Soon some of the members of our new church began to come to our home group, where signs and wonders were happening pretty regularly. Healings, visions, prophetic words, deliverances, and the presence of God flowed powerfully in that season. Word started getting out, and more people were coming – even those we didn't know were led to come.

Between my husband's healing, his heavenly encounter, and my gift of faith, this had been a total God set up, which prepared us for this great move of God. It had been totally God's idea, and we just came along for the ride of a lifetime!

The new pastor and some of the elders didn't believe in the manifestations they heard were happening at our home, and the pastor came to tell us we needed to stop what we were doing. Sometime during that evening, the Holy Spirit grabbed hold of the pastor and that very Sunday, he was preaching on the need for the Baptism of the Holy Spirit.

From there, the Holy Spirit spread even more in the revival that was birthed in our living room. Signs and wonders were commonplace during this season, the supernatural power of God would fall, and amazing miracles would take place every time we met. Eventually, we all were forced out of that church because of the move of God and launched out to start a new church.

During worship, the presence of God would fall so powerfully that demons would continually manifest in our midst because they couldn't remain silent in the power of His presence. As a result, I became part of the deliverance team.

One morning a woman attended our service. I heard the Lord tell me she was a heroin addict and to set her free. When I asked her about her addictions, she replied she was, and told me she wanted to be set free. The Lord so delivered her that she never even had withdrawals. That night, she came back to the evening service with another woman who also wanted to be set free. With such powerful meetings and miraculous encounters, this revival lasted three years.

We needed to move into a larger home Sunday evenings as the Spirit moved so powerfully, that many were being added. Until, the pastor decided it was getting too large and stopped the meetings, as he felt the group needed more order.

The Spirit was grieved and soon stopped moving as He had been. Some of us knew it wasn't a good decision to stop meetings where the Lord's presence was moving so powerfully. Those who were attending the Sunday evening meetings were so hungry for the things of the Spirit and the supernatural realm. After that revival period ended, I went into a *deep* grieving. I didn't understand what happened, as we were newbies to the Spirit. I didn't understand *why* it was over in just three years, as I had never experienced a move of God before.

I continually pressed into the Lord until He told me why it ended. He said it was because there was no *holiness* in our lives. Things like control, offenses, fear, jealousy, power struggles, unforgiveness, gossip, and all these types of sins had grieved the Spirit and prevented Him from moving. I made up my mind that very day to never be part of another revival until holiness was produced in my life. I didn't want a revival that began and ended but desired one that would be permanently sustained.

Many people ended up leaving the church in conflicts and divisions. Those of us who were there in the beginning of that revival saw things that weren't right, and in our immaturity, we gossiped and became judgmental. Several of our close friends decided to leave, but we stayed – until I was accused of being a false prophet and was asked to leave the church. This was such a painful time in my life, and I was so wounded and broken.

We started another home group, which met for about a year, and the Lord began dealing with me about my own part in what happened there. He impressed me to write the pastor a letter asking him to forgive me for judging him, gossiping, and my lack of love. In the letter, I told him I forgave him for all the hurt he caused me and never expected to hear from him. From that obedience, I knew I was set free and could now move forward.

A few days after sending the letter, the pastor appeared at my front door and asked me to forgive him for the hurt he caused me. He told me I would be welcome back at his church, but I replied that it was time for us to move on. I asked if he would bless us to find another church, and he prayed for me. After that, we started attending a newer church in an adjacent town.

In more recent years, I have learned we need to be responsible for cleaning up our messes. That letter to the pastor was a pivotal point in my walk with the Lord and became a great learning experience for all future church relationships. Years later, I had to do the same thing with another pastor I had judged. Since that day, it has been indelibly imprinted on my heart to leave a church the right way and ask for the blessing of the pastor before moving from one church to the next.

Do not leave a church without a blessing from the pastor; for God blesses those who understand authority and leave the right way.

This is a very important secret of the Kingdom that many don't understand. It's all about having the right heart, even if you don't get the pastor's blessing because they are unwilling. God will look at *your* willingness in asking them and bless you for it.

My strongest attribute is I am passionate about learning and personal growth; and hungry for more of the things of the Kingdom. I became teachable, which is another quality crucial to advancing in the Kingdom.

We need to become teachable in order to advance in the Kingdom of God.

A personal quest for holiness became my lifelong passion. Later in my walk, the Lord told me to replace the word *holiness* with *transformation,* and transformation became the passionate pursuit of my heart for myself, others, and regions. For transformation leads us deeper into holiness.

What had been my greatest weakness, in areas needing such transformation, became my greatest strength, in having a heart for transformation. That's exactly what God does, and He is so good at it!

As we read the chapters in this book, we will see how the Lord opened the door to *many* Kingdom secrets being *revealed* and the lessons necessary to be able to walk out those secrets.

WHY ARE YOU TELLING ME?

The journey to write this book began sixteen years ago, and I could never have imagined where it would take me.

My journey is two-fold: The first is being a woman with a call of God on my life, and the other is a journey to understanding divine order, the government of God, and how to go deeper into His Kingdom. These came with a high price attached to them that could only be birthed from being purified through the fire of the Spirit. Only by walking through such fires, will we fully come to understand the revelations I will be sharing here.

My church experience had been where women could lead either Sunday school classes for children or women, or lead a women's group. They could not be part of the leadership within a church, teach men, or preach from a pulpit because of the interpretation of some bible verses regarding women. Because of this teaching, I began to lead various women's groups over the course of the eighteen years *prior* to the eventful moment I am about to share.

At this time, I was co-leading a women's group in my church, where the Spirit of the Lord would move powerfully every week in worship, visions, the gifts, the prophetic, healing, and in the Word of God. One evening the Lord gave me several scripture verses and told me something that changed the direction of my life.

These verses were:

> *"And He gave the apostles, the prophets, the evangelists, the pastors and teachers to equip the saints for the work of the ministry, for building up the body of Christ, until we all attain to the unity of the faith and of the knowledge of the Son of God to mature manhood, to the measure of the stature of the fullness of Christ, so that we may no longer be children, tossed to and fro by the waves and carried about by every wind of doctrine, by human cunning, by craftiness in deceitful schemes."*
> Ephesians 4:11–14 (ESV)

The other one was:

> *"And God has appointed in the church, first apostles, second prophets, third teachers, then miracles, then gifts of healings, helps, administrations, various kinds of tongues."*
> I Corinthians 12:28 (NASB)

I had read these verses so many times prior, but in reading them that night, the Spirit spoke to me this secret:

"I never intended My Church to be led by pastors, but by the order of the five–fold ministry."

This was a great secret that would change my life!

My immediate response was, "Lord, why are you telling me this? What can I do about it?" You need to understand where I was during that season. I couldn't comprehend *why* He was telling *me* this and couldn't help feeling He should be telling someone who could actually bring about the changes needed.

That night, I came to the understanding of how the Church needed to be restored to the divine order set forth in these verses. The purpose of this shift, according to the Word of God, was to equip people for the work of the ministry, to build them up in the Body of Christ, and to help them walk in maturity. *Then*, they would walk in the fullness of Christ and no longer be tossed to and fro by false teachings that would lead them astray.

Also, that night, I realized the current form of church structure needed to change. I was overwhelmed with, *"How in the world is this going to happen?"*

Little did I know all that was to come!

WHAT HAPPENED?

What happened to the Church? What happened that we are no longer walking in the divine order set forth in the Word of God? I do not judge any of what I am relating from history, but only letting us know the events leading up to how we ended up where we are today. History gives us the opportunity to look back, learn, and gain understanding.

Over the centuries, Satan has tried to destroy the plan of God. He tried to kill the male babies during the time of Moses, as well as the male babies during the time of Jesus' birth. That didn't accomplish what he hoped for, so Satan tried persecuting Jesus, but that only made Him stronger. What he couldn't do from the outside, he accomplished from the inside. With Jesus, it took one of his own to bring Him to the cross when Judas betrayed Him for the gold coins. This was Jesus' plan all along to die, but Satan was able to accomplish it from within. Since persecution of the Church only made *them* stronger, Satan accomplished what he couldn't do from the outside, from the inside once again.

What I am sharing is based on the research I did while trying to understand how the Church government we read about, in the New Testament, was lost.

It started in 306 A.D., when the Roman emperor, Constantine, was persecuting the Christians and killing them. He served the pagan gods of Rome, but in 312 A.D., converted to Christianity and decided to unify the religions of his day into a new universal church. He blended elements from these religions into one, thus changing the Church from the New Testament type of government, to one of his own making.

He hated the Jews and their practices and disallowed followers of Christ to participate in the Jewish feasts, which had been common practice since the beginning of Christianity. By this, Satan was able to destroy our Jewish roots, as Jesus, all the apostles, and the disciples were Jewish and celebrated the Jewish feasts. At that time, many Gentiles were also participating in the feasts.

Constantine created a new *universal* church, and since he was used to being the only ultimate authority, he did away with the apostle and prophet, and put priests into place who served his universal church. The Council of Nicea in 325 A.D. *replaced* the biblical Passover with Easter, and Constantine forbade Easter to be celebrated at the same time as Passover. Celebrating Passover, or the Jewish feasts, came with *serious* consequences.

The Easter celebration, during Constantine's period, had been a popular Roman holiday celebrating the fertility rites of their goddess, Eostre. Constantine combined the day of Eostre's celebration, Jesus' crucifixion, and His rising, together on Easter. Jesus *actually* died and rose again on the Feast of Passover, which they were no longer allowed to celebrate.

He disallowed participating in the biblical Sabbath which began at Friday evening sundown and ended Saturday at sundown. He also disallowed the Jewish Shabbat which was held every Friday evening at sundown. Constantine would not allow *any* Jewish elements to remain part of his new Christianity. He also expressed his blatant animosity and desire, "*to separate ourselves from the detestable company of the Jews*" (*Vita Constantini iii, 18*).

"*Mithra, the Light of the World, is an ancient sun god identified with Sol Invictus, who was born on December 25th.*"
(truthbeknown.com/mithra.htm)

The Romans worshipped Mithra, and since they were used to celebrating their sun god's birth on December 25th, Constantine made this same date a Christian holiday for the birth of Christ. Once again we see the melding of the two religions to become a new universal church.

Bible scholars have studied the biblical facts surrounding Jesus' birth. Shepherds, in the biblical account of His birth, were no longer in the fields with their sheep during December, but returned home for the winter by the end of October until the following spring. They also looked at how many months Elizabeth was pregnant with John the Baptist, as well as how many months Mary was pregnant when she visited Elizabeth. The determination, based on these facts, put Jesus' actual birth somewhere in early fall, before the shepherds left the fields with their sheep to return home for the winter until spring. *(www.bibleinfo.com/en/questions/when-was-jesus-born)*

Constantine appeased those in Rome with his new Christian beliefs by combining Christianity with their Roman idols' sacred dates and practices. He made Christianity palatable for himself and the Romans, and consequently, what Constantine put into place is where the Church has been for centuries.

The Church government found in the New Testament was now a thing of the past! The entire church was under Constantine's rule, and anyone opposing the ordinances of his universal church was *not* tolerated.

This is how we moved from the New Testament form of government to what *we* know today, as our biblical holidays and current form of Church government. We have had these traditions for centuries, and all I am conveying here is the *history* of how we arrived to where we currently *are* in the Church.

We entered a period called The Dark Ages, until a monk named Martin Luther, in 1517 A.D., put a decree on the door of the universal church that stated salvation is by faith and not by works. This *began* a reformation of the Church! There have been many other reformations that have taken place since the day of Martin Luther, where the great Protestant movement began. Each reformation restored another significant truth which had been lost to the church.

In the last few centuries, God began a process of restoring the five–fold ministries to the Church. Priests led the universal church for 1200 years, while the biblical five–fold offices had been lost. Even though these truths have always remained, they had been hidden from the Church until God began a restoration of pastors and teachers during the Protestant movement. This move brought biblical teaching, revelation, and understanding back to the Church. In more recent days, the healing evangelist movement was followed by the restoration of the prophet, and currently we see the apostle being raised up.

Reformation is eternal and always brings us back to God's original design.

I have come to realize revivals *always* have a beginning and an end date, but just like in the days of Martin Luther's refor-mation, salvation by grace has never been lost. What we actual-ly need is *complete* reformation back to biblical precepts, re-storing God's original design for man, the Church, and world.

Until the apostle is fully functional, the Church won't be what it is meant to be. The apostles need to take their spiritual place as originally intended. When these five–fold ministries are placed back into divine order, I believe we will see an explo-sion of the Church impacting nations once again. We will be given tremendous authority and power, and God's glory will be restored to the Body of Christ. We are now in the transition stage of this restoration process, in those Churches which have one again, embraced this Bible–based New Testament form of government.

The Lord is restoring them in reverse order for a reason. The apostle is being restored last because they are the foundation at the bottom holding all the other five–fold offices in place, as the servant leader. This is the reverse order of how the world does government and leadership, which is top–centered down. The Church needs to embrace and transition from its current pastor–centered leadership, which is not the original design of the New Testament, to having the apostle once again at the foundation leading from the bottom up.

After a ministry trip, we had the opportunity to visit a city in Cyprus and went to an ancient Roman amphitheater. The entire group went down the stairs to the bottom of the theater facing the ocean. Because my knee was hurting, I chose not to do all those stairs and stayed at the top. When they reached the bottom, everyone took their turn praying.

The Lord showed me, because my father is Italian, He wanted me to stand and repent on behalf of Constantine and what he had done to the Church by changing from the New Testament form of government. After doing so, I made declarations which spoke to the reformation of the government of God being reestablished in the Church.

When I was done, there was a heavenly portal which opened over my head. I could hear heavenly wind instruments I can't explain because I had never heard anything like them before. Some of the others in our group heard the voices of angels singing. The music lasted as long as we were in the amphi-theater. It was truly a supernatural experience, which has been permanently etched upon my heart.

I am confident those churches, who have an ear to hear, are transitioning back to the original plan of God set forth in His

Word – and what a glorious day that will be!

It's very important to not walk in any kind of criticism or judgment toward those who are resistant to making these changes. It's very difficult to change after being indoctrinated by 1,700 years of wrong teaching. It's going to take a move of God to bring us out of the deception we have been in! Let's pray for our brothers and sisters to hear the Spirit, who is wooing us back to walking in His divine order.

**Pray and walk in love toward those who oppose us,
as this is the way of the Kingdom of God!**

Lord, I declare those who come to understand Kingdom principles will walk in heavenly revelation as it pertains to returning to God's original design, biblical principles, transformation, divine order, and walking in love toward those who oppose them! In Jesus' name, Amen.

SECRET KINGDOM PRINCIPLES

**Do not leave a church without a blessing from the pastor, for
God blesses those who understand authority
and leave the right way.**

We need to become teachable in order to advance
in the Kingdom of God.

"I never intended My Church to be led by pastors, but
by the order of the five-fold ministries."

Reformation is eternal and always brings
us back to God's original design.

Pray and walk in love toward those who oppose us,
as this is the way of the Kingdom of God!

Daniel 2:22 He reveals the deep and secret things...

Chapter 2
YOU WANT ME TO DO WHAT?

"For I am a man under authority, with soldiers under me."
Matthew 8:9 (KJB)

I had major issues in my life that needed healing and over the years, I had been through so much inner healing, but the Lord knew there were more things still needing such transformation.

Sometime later, the Lord called me to start another women's group outside the church in our capital city. I brought one of the women in my church with me as part of my leadership team, and this ministry was part of a national ministry with existing state leaders in place.

At that time, the Lord gave me another verse, which once again reset the course of my life. Throughout the years, I have experienced so many resets in my journey. This passage is found in Matthew 8, where the Roman centurion sought out Jesus to heal his servant. Jesus stated that He had found no one with that kind of faith in all of Israel. There was one particular verse that jumped off the page when I read it. It was what the centurion told Jesus.

"For I am a man under authority, with soldiers under me."
Matthew 8:9 (KJB)

A centurion was a Roman officer in command of a hundred men within a legion of 6,000 soldiers. He had command over his hundred and reported to others in higher rank. I noticed the centurion *first* stated he was *under* authority before telling Jesus he had authority over others. I heard the Lord tell me another secret in my spirit:

**"Until you learn how to walk *under* authority,
you will not be given *great* authority."**

I could tell the woman who was the state leader of that woman's ministry didn't like me. I responded just like I always did when facing any type of conflict. My modus operandi was to pull back, put walls up, and keep quiet around them, while at the same time complaining to others and becoming judgmental of those in opposition to me. When the leader made it quite clear she didn't like me, she made life quite difficult for me. I really wanted out, but the Lord reminded me He had called me to this and I needed to stay to walk through this season. The leader tried to give the lead of this new ministry to someone else, but it failed. At the last moment, the person she assigned to take the lead ended up giving it back to me. But even at that, it turned out to be in name only. She had a strong controlling and manipulative spirit and would run roughshod over my leadership, challenging me at every decision and in everything I felt the Holy Spirit was saying. She also worked behind my back with my leadership team to undermine me. Because she was not my choice but was put in that place by the state leader, I was forced to walk through this season.

At the same time, the Lord called us to leave our current church to help someone we knew start a new church, as we have always been called to new churches for a season. However, the pastors of this church walked in legalism, and people began leaving the church. The Lord wouldn't let me leave because He had something to teach me by staying. Not recognizing it at the time, there was a common thread being woven through these circumstances.

When everything is coming at me at the same time, it becomes too much for me to bear. That's when I'm ready for transformation, and the Lord knows this about me. During this highly miserable time, the Lord led me in I Samuel 21–28 to the story of King Saul and young David, who had been anointed to be the new king. Saul was persecuting David and chasing him into caves to kill him, while David was constantly running for his life.

I began to see how David walked in the midst of this trial, with honor and love for a king who was trying to murder him. Several times, David had the opportunity to kill Saul, but only cut the hem of his garment – and felt guilty about even doing that. When Saul chased David into those caves, the Lord used those cave experiences in David's life to mold him and transform his character, by teaching him how to honor an unjust king. We can't even fathom living such a life, but this example was used in my life to bring about a greatly needed paradigm shift. David never spoke against the king but honored his position of authority, even though Samuel had anointed David to be the new king. Now, this is something to aspire to!

At that time, I did not understand the value of *caves* in my life, nor did I recognize that I was in a cave of the Lord's making. It was a test tailored just for me, in order to be transformed from responses that didn't line up with the Word of God. I needed to come out of my strongholds into freedom.

Wow, the Lord spoke to me about all the authority issues I was dealing with in the ministry and church. He didn't want me to respond the way I always did in the past. Instead, He gave me a new way – the way of David! I knew I had to stop pulling back, putting up walls, judging them, and gossiping. Their animosity toward me and their harsh ways were difficult to deal with, but I began to understand what the apostle Paul said, in Philippians 2:3, about esteeming others higher than ourselves. This revealed a powerful secret:

**Learn to honor those for the authority – wrong or
right – they have been given, esteeming them
higher than ourselves.**

The kind of honor David walked in toward Saul was one of the most critical character building attributes he carried into his new kingdom, and the caves had prepared him to be a righteous ruler. The Lord had a purpose for David's cave experiences, just as He does for our *caves*. These cave experiences are the very thing that shaped David's life as he was learning how to honor a king who hated him enough to see him dead.

To be quite honest, the natural man in me would battle these thoughts, *"They don't deserve honor for what they are doing or saying."* I would have to be reminded of David and Saul and begin all over again. This was not a quick work as it took quite a while to learn to walk in honor toward my leaders and to react in kindness when harshness was coming toward me. I was always being reminded of how Jesus responded toward those crying out for His death and nailed Him to a cross:

> *"Father, forgive them for they know not what they do."*
> Luke 23:34

No matter how much we would like to, we can't rush or skip any steps through this process, because it's *this* very thing that prepares us for promotion from God. We would much rather get on with the vision God has given us, but after we go through this process and look back, we will see and understand what God accomplished in our lives to prepare us for the next season we found ourselves in.

His vision and call on our lives may be huge, but God is not concerned. He knows it will not happen until He has prepared our inner life and character to match this great call. So, like David, we need to learn to embrace our *cave* experiences. We must stay hidden until we are transformed. The *caves* are what *prepares* us for the great destiny we have! The duration of how long we stay hidden is in direct proportion to how quickly we submit and learn what we need to during this season. David spent years in his caves!

This was a great time of learning how to walk in a new way with those who were over me. It was also time to learn a new way to deal with the one usurping *my* leadership. Finally, the time had come when I became healthier and realized the need to confront this leader, instead of dealing with her in my old ways. I was planning to speak to her, but I heard in my spirit, "Will you take the low road and bow to get out of My way?" I answered, "Yes," and the Lord gave me instructions that I should wash all my leaders' feet. Shortly after that foot washing, I received a letter of resignation from this leader, and just like that, she was gone.

If we humble ourselves and obey what the Lord tells us to do, He will work on our behalf.

Little did I understand this unusual way the Lord worked, and contrary to how I normally do things, prepared me for the next assignment He would lead me into. Soon after that experience, the Lord spoke to me that this season was over and I was to leave. Once we learn the lessons He wants to instill in our character, He moves us out of our *cave* and into the next season and assignment. With my term up, I handed the ministry over to other leaders and moved on. Shortly after that, I was also released from the church, as the Lord told me my season was over.

After going through those trials, I now understood how to be *under authority*, no matter what those authorities were doing. I also learned how to honor leaders, even if I felt they didn't deserve the honor. This *secret* was extremely pivotal and important for the next season and assignment in my life on this journey to understanding divine order. The secret? Here it is:

If we don't learn to truly honor *every* authority over us, we will not be able to carry the greater Kingdom authority for the next season.

My capacity for walking in authority had *greatly* increased by going through and passing this valuable Kingdom lesson.

WHAT'S IT GOING TO TAKE?

The next season I entered would teach me to truly understand how to be *in authority*. While leading that women's ministry in our capital city, I read a book about regional transformation and felt a strong call to start a regional ministry. I came to understand that unless the powers of darkness are removed over a region, it is very difficult for a move of God to come, as they hinder that move through the legal access they have in that region. (This will be covered in a later chapter).

Reluctant to start it and needing many confirmations, I finally obeyed. While in that women's ministry, I met several women leaders in the city and felt they would make good team members for the new regional transformation ministry. One was a local co–pastor who walked in the prophetic and the other led an intercessory prayer ministry in the city. The last team member was a prophetic intercessor I had walked with for thirty years and trusted. *All* of us were women!

The Lord had given me a vision for the city, but as we met, I eventually came to understand these great women leaders had their own calling and passions they brought into the ministry. Consequently, the vision and strategies given to *me* for the capital city were not being accomplished in the spirit realm.

These women were – and still are – great ministers, doing good work in the city. My mistake was I moved ahead of the Lord in selecting those I thought would be spiritual assets to the call and vision He gave me. I didn't wait for those He selected and this is always a mistake! My friend and I were led in one direction and the other women were led in other directions. It wasn't working, but I didn't make a change for a full year until I came to the understanding we were not fulfilling what the Lord had shown me for the region.

Sometimes we just have to experience things in order to learn Kingdom ways. This was a time The Lord was teaching me another secret.

We need to wait for Him to build the team with those He has called to support the vision He gave, and not to appoint those *we* choose.

During the first year of the reginal ministry, the Lord orchestrated some divine connections for my life and ministry. I connected with a woman who had a statewide regional ministry and she invited me to a conference at her church. From this conference, my husband and I met her senior leader, heard him speak, and heard the Lord call us to begin attending this church, even though it was quite a distance from our home. We were amazed at the kind of authority and government this man of God demonstrated, and the Lord knew I needed to be there.

The Lord told me we would be there for a season to learn about family and the new wine. He also told me that He wanted to show me the new wineskin for the call He had on my life. He said, since all I saw modeled was the old wineskin, old wine was all I would be able to produce.

During one of the conferences at our new church, a man turned around and introduced himself to me. He walked heavily in the prophetic and began to minister to me over the course of many months. After that time, he was called to come alongside to support the ministry and became a new member of the regional team. I also met another man who had leaders' meetings within the capital city and walked in the apostolic over that city. I began attending his gatherings and shortly was invited to become the moderator over their monthly leadership meetings. I felt strongly that he was to be part of the ministry and he joined us.

With my prophetic intercessor friend and these two men, we formed a regional group of apostolic and prophetic team members. A man I never met, walked up at one leadership meeting and told me the Lord had spoken to him to give me office space in his building near the capitol.

God was all over this assignment! Between God choosing the team members and His provision of an office space, He had it covered. It's amazing what happens when we follow the Lord's leading and wait for His divine appointments to orchestrate what He has called us to do.

Never, in my wildest imagination, did I ever think I would lead a group with men on the team, especially with my current understanding of a woman's limitations. That was about to change when I heard the Lord call me to an apostolic role. I replied, "How can this be? I am a woman." Because of my past teachings, I didn't tell *anyone* about my calling until I received a prophetic word from a man, confirming my call to the apostolic. God is *always* faithful to confirm His Word to us! He also knew I needed that confirmation to come from a man.

Because of the teaching about women I was indoctrinated by, the Lord had to do some work to rearrange my thinking to set me straight. Thankfully, my husband, the senior leader of our church, and the two men in the ministry saw the call of God on my life and believed in Galatians 3:28, that in Christ there is neither male nor female. They were such an encouragement to me regarding this apostolic calling I received. The Lord was faithful to lead me to two books that radically transformed my life and confronted my thinking on this *woman* issue. One was written by Danny Silk called *Powerful and Free: Confronting the Glass Ceiling for Women in the Church.* The other book was by Kris Vallotton called *Fashioned to Reign: Empowering Women to Fulfill Their Divine Destiny.*

I came to understand the Church has held some wrong views on women based on verses meant specifically for certain women in *that particular* church who were causing trouble – just as He dealt with certain men who were causing trouble in other churches. I learned there were two women apostles mentioned in the New Testament. One was Junia, and the other was Priscilla, whose husband was Aquilla. For the New Testament to put a woman's name before the husband was not the custom of the day, as they *always* put the man's name before the woman's in New Testament times. The book explained the reason her name was probably put before her husband's was she had the greater anointing in an apostolic role. I learned when the Church embraces the call of women into leadership roles and in the five-fold ministry, we will see the greatest harvest, power, and glory being restored to the Church in this next season. If you want to learn more about this issue of women in the Church and leadership roles, please read these books. They have so much *more* revelation contained in them than I want to address here.

When God created male and female in Genesis 1:26–27, it says He created them in His image. *"So God created mankind in His own image, in the image of God He created them, male and female He created them."* God created man first and breathed within man His full image and attributes, meaning: *'qualities or features regarded as a characteristic or inherent part of some-one.'* When He created woman from man, He removed Adam's rib to create Eve, but also some of those attributes He had given man, and put them into woman. This gave man and woman *different* attributes of God that now displayed His *full* image. Thereby only *together,* expressing the *complete* image of God. He created *them* in *His* likeness and meant for them to become *one,* with complimentary attributes and characteristics.

Genesis 1:26–27 says, they – male and female, were called to rule and have dominion together, which gives us a beautiful picture of God's original intent. That joint dominion was lost after Adam and Eve sinned, but Jesus came to restore their dominion through the cross. As it says in Galatians 3:13, Jesus came to redeem us from the curse by becoming a curse for us. It's time to restore that which was lost, with man and woman walking in harmony as God originally designed. Once again, *together,* expressing the *full* image and character of God as *He* intended from the beginning. Genesis 2:18 says that it was not good for man to be alone so God created woman as a suitable helper, meaning *'right for someone.'* Woman was intended to both compliment and complete man, thus becoming *one*! God had created this beautiful, loving plan for them. It's time for a paradigm shift to expose the work of the enemy who has been deceiving us about God's *true* purpose for man and woman, to keep us *powerless* and no longer a threat to his kingdom!

I am thankful for my leaders up north and also for my senior leaders where I currently live, who have embraced the truth that women can be anything God calls them to be!

This *new* team the Lord formed in the regional ministry began to teach me what true unity, authority, and submission looked like. While I was in the leadership meetings for the city, I honored the apostolic leader, submitting under the authority of his leadership of that ministry. While he was in my meetings, he honored me and put himself under my authority as leader of this ministry.

Learn to lay aside our own personal vision and call in order to submit under the leader.

Both of us were submitting to the vision of the other, depending on whose sphere of authority we were in at the two meetings. There was also complete unity between the apostolic and prophetic team members. Each one knew their call and role, and walked in such honor, love, and submission. We esteemed each other better than ourselves, as the Word admonishes us to do. During this time, we were seeing the *value* and need for each member of the team, as we moved with great authority in what the Lord gave us to do, both prophetically and in the things He revealed to us for the region. I called them my dream team! Finally, I understood the difference between *us* appointing people to positions rather than God putting them into place. I am so thankful to have had this team because it was in this season I learned how to depend on both the prophetic and apostolic authority to accomplish the assignment for the transformation of the region I was given. Great secrets of the Kingdom were gleaned in this season, concerning what true submission and unity looked like.

The Lord showed me the first team I had for the first year in ministry represented today's Church, where everyone has a call on their life, follows that call, and everywhere they go they bring this call with them. These women were great leaders, but didn't understand how to submit to another leader's vision and truly come *under* someone else's authority. This is one reason why churches don't operate in honor, glory, and power. They don't understand divine order, proper alignment, and being in right relationship *under* authority.

The second team represented the new, emerging apostolic Church where each team member served the vision and call of the apostle. Here is another great Kingdom secret:

Learn to recognize whose sphere of authority we are under.

This is where great power, glory, honor, and divine exploits for assignment come from, in understanding how to truly come *under authority*.

Lord, I declare those reading this book will come into new understanding of how to come under authority in order to walk in great authority. Also, how to come under another's vision and calling in order to fulfill God's purposes on the earth. In Jesus' name, Amen.

SECRET KINGDOM PRINCIPLES

"Until you learn how to walk *under* authority, you will not be given *great* authority."

Learn to honor those for the authority – wrong or right – they have been given, esteeming them higher than ourselves.

If we humble ourselves and obey what the Lord tells us to do, He will work on our behalf.

If we don't learn to truly honor every authority over us, we will not be able to carry the greater Kingdom authority for the next season.

We need to wait for Him to build the team with those He has called to support the vision He gave, and not to appoint those we choose.

Learn to lay aside our own personal vision and call in order to submit under the leader.

Learn to recognize whose sphere of authority we are under.

Chapter 3

EXTRAORDINARY TIMES PART 1

"Consider it pure joy, my brothers and sisters, whenever you face trials of many kinds, because you know that the testing of your faith produces perseverance. Let perseverance finish its work so that you may be mature and complete, not lacking anything."
James 1:2–4

FROM DREAM TO DESTINY

Destiny is like a father who had a nine-year-old son who came to him saying, "Father, I am ready to drive the family car and I'm asking you to give me the keys." The father replied, "Son, you are not ready to drive a car, as I am really concerned you might hurt others or yourself. Rest assured, when I see you are mature enough to drive the family car, I will gladly hand you the keys." The son went away *very* upset because he *believed* he was already mature enough.

The Lord gave me a powerful revelation of a Kingdom secret about how to go *from our dream to destiny* through the story of Joseph, son of Jacob. This bible story reveals how we need to respond to those over us and to those who have wronged us. This teaching transformed my understanding about things that happened in my life from that point on. Another secret was revealed:

**Tests of life are the way of the King to
prepare us for our destiny.**

Everyone goes through tests of life, but many people never get past their pain. Sadly, they just keep going around the mountain over and over again, never fulfilling the great destiny the Lord has for them.

> *"For the grace of God has appeared that offers salvation
> to all people. It teaches us to say, 'No,' to ungodliness
> and worldly passions, and to live self-controlled,
> upright and Godly lives in this present age."*
> Titus 2:11–12

Have we really learned to say, "No," to every form of ungodliness in our life? It doesn't just mean we no longer get drunk or do drugs but also need to say, "No," to anger, envy, offenses, unforgiveness, the desire for platforms, and so much more. It's God's grace that teaches us to say, "No," to all these ungodly sins and worldly passions; to live self-controlled and upright.

> *"I know what it is to be in need, and I know what it is to*

*have plenty. I have learned the secret of being content
in any and every situation, whether well fed or hungry,
whether living in plenty or in want."*
Philippians 4:12

Learn to be content in every circumstance we find ourselves in – pleasant or difficult.

Have we learned this secret for our own lives – being content in *every* circumstance we find ourselves in? Being content in both the pleasant circumstances and the *difficult* ones? Yes, it is possible! I remember a time in my life when I couldn't even imagine doing that. I would tell the Lord, *"I don't know this secret!"* At the time, my circumstances determined if I was doing well or not, and my emotions were enslaved to them.

Jesus told Simon Peter in Luke 22:31, that Satan asked if he could sift Peter like wheat. Just look at the destiny Peter moved into, after he was tested by denying Christ three times. A great transformation took place in his life, and he became one of the greats of the Bible. All the tests he faced prepared him to be the apostle he became, and he made Church history. Also, remember after Job was tested and how he received double what Satan had taken from him? Clearly, we see examples throughout the Bible of those who were tested and the blessings that came from passing those tests.

Learn to move beyond the pain in our life in order to walk healed and whole.

We also really need to grab hold of and understand what these tests produce in our lives. We must begin to cooperate with them so we, like Joseph, can fulfill our own great destiny.

God may give us a dream or a prophetic word, or we may have passions and desires in our heart. God may even speak to us directly about our destiny and assignments. Satan does his best to rob us of that dream or word. He *tried* to do that to Job and Peter! John 10:10 says, Satan has come to steal, kill, and destroy our lives, but he doesn't have to succeed if we learn and grow from our tests of life.

There is a *great* purpose for passing these tests, as God uses our trials to bring us to maturity. We know this because the Word teaches us in James 1:2–4, to consider it pure joy when we face trials. It's the testing of our faith that produces perseverance in us, so that we can be mature and complete, lacking nothing. There are tests of life we all experience and can learn from, by looking at the life of Joseph; tests we must all pass in order to become mature vessels prepared to fulfill our dreams.

Let's look at the life of Joseph in Genesis 37:2–5, for a deeper understanding of his life and the tests he needed to pass in order to fulfill his dreams.

"This is the account of Jacob's family line. Joseph, a young man of seventeen was tending the flocks with his brothers, the sons of Bilhah and the sons of Zilpah, his father's wives and he brought their father a bad report about them. Now Israel (Jacob) loved Joseph more than any of his other sons, because he had been born to him in his old age; and he made an ornate robe for him. When his brothers saw that their father loved him more than any of them, they hated him and couldn't speak a kind

word to him. Joseph had a dream and when he told it to his brothers, they hated him all the more."

Joseph didn't use wisdom in flaunting his ornate coat, tattling on his brothers, or sharing his dreams. He was a teenager and was young in his thinking and understanding. He had some pride issues that needed maturing, as well as character training. The truth is, so do we!

Let's put ourselves in the brothers' shoes here. Their father gave Joseph a coat, which not only signified him being the favorite, but the brothers were constantly reminded that he was in a higher status than they were. He spied and tattled on his brothers and felt the need to tell them his dreams, even though they made it very clear how they felt about him. That sure wasn't wisdom!

If we were one of his brothers, I wonder how we might have felt growing up with him. We know Joseph had a great call and destiny on his life, but in the natural, all the brothers could see was what was happening to them and blamed him.

THE TEST OF BEING HATED AND MISUNDERSTOOD

In light of Joseph's life, let's look at the first test he experienced, one we all experience throughout life: being misunderstood and hated by others. Here, Joseph's brothers saw him as the enemy and hated him. When we find ourselves in this position, Satan wants us to have the wrong response to knock us off–track from the path that leads to the dream or calling the

Lord has given us. His goal is to keep us *stuck* in pain, which keeps us from being able to walk with power and authority.

Satan uses the tools of unforgiveness, bitterness, or resentment and wants us to have negative responses, like anger, rejection, defensiveness, or retaliation. Rejection will play havoc in our lives if we don't deal with it and will keep us in a prison that will even effect our health.

In Genesis 37:6–8 (NASB), Joseph had a dream; and when he told his brothers, they hated him all the more.

> *"He said to them, 'Please listen to this dream which I have*
> *had; for behold, we were binding sheaves in the field, and*
> *lo, my sheaf rose up and also stood erect; and behold, your*
> *sheaves gathered around and bowed down to my sheaf.'*
> *Then his brothers said to him, 'Are you actually going to*
> *reign over us? Or are you really going to rule over us?'*
> *So they hated him even more for his dreams*
> *and for his words."*

We really need to be careful who we share our dreams with. This test is not just the test of being misunderstood, but hated, and it's not usually the unbelievers who will hate you when you speak of your dream. The enemy has a plan to stop you and uses people to do it if you play this game with him. He wants to render you ineffective and will try to shut you down by any means possible. Sadly, many Christians fall into this trap by sharing dreams with people they shouldn't.

In my own immaturity and early in my walk with the Lord, whenever I received revelations, dreams, or prophetic words, I would get so excited and feel the need to tell everyone. That didn't work well for me, as I received a lot of rejection and jealousy from others.

We need the Lord's wisdom to keep things to ourselves unless He gives us someone in our life who is *safe*, who will fan the flames of that dream and not douse it with water! At the same time, the Lord is trying to produce unconditional love in us, right in the midst of people who hate us. In Luke 6:27, Jesus tells us to bless our enemies and do good to those who hate us.

Later, Joseph had another dream that would bring him to another test.

THE TEST OF JEALOUSY

"Then he had another dream, and he told it to his brothers. 'Listen,' he said, 'I had another dream, and this time the sun and moon and eleven stars were bowing down to me.' When he told his father, as well as his brothers, his father rebuked him and said, 'What is this dream you had? Will your mother and I and your brothers actually come and bow down to the ground before you?' His brothers were jealous of him."
Genesis 37:9–10

A test in life we all have is others will be jealous of us. His brothers envied him, his place with their father, his coat, and his dreams.

In I Samuel 18, Saul became jealous of David and tried to kill him after David came home and the crowd was singing about David killing more people than Saul.

"A heart at peace gives life to the body, but envy rots the bones."

Proverbs 14:30

Envy can cause many health problems and is a common problem for mankind. We just don't understand the correlation between sin and the many health issues they cause. Science has found the correlation between stress, fear, bitterness, and the health issues they cause.

"For jealousy arouses a husband's fury, and he will show no mercy when he takes revenge."
Proverbs 6:34

Another version of this verse says, Jealousy is the rage of a man, and he has fits of rage. When Saul became jealous of David, his fury raged with no mercy. Saul began to seek revenge on David by planning to kill him.

God wants us to learn, in the midst of this test, how to rejoice in another man's blessings. Jealousy not only needs to be removed from *our* lives, but we also need to learn how to walk in God's perfect peace in the midst of jealousy directed toward us. We must learn to walk in a lifestyle of forgiveness because this will lead us into peace in the midst of our storms of life.

There is no place for jealousy in the Kingdom of God, if we want to walk in great authority.

Years ago, I didn't think very highly of myself and constantly compared myself to others. The result was, I always came up short in my own mind. This caused jealousy to rise up in me toward others. I came to realize, because of the unhealed areas of my life, I couldn't receive the love of the Father or encounter

His love. I was fertile ground for jealousy, but God was faithful to lead me to those who could minister to those broken places in me. Be careful we don't mask our jealousy by believing we just don't like someone. We need to ask the Holy Spirit to examine our heart to see if the reason we have those feelings of dislike for someone might be jealousy, and then repent.

THE PIT TEST

What did Joseph's brothers do with their hate and jealousy? Joseph's father sent him once again to see how his brothers and sheep were doing in the field, but they had enough of his tattling, his fancy coat, and farfetched dreams.

"But they saw him in the distance, and before he reached them, they plotted to kill him. They began to conspire against him to kill him and throw him into a pit."
Genesis 37:18

This is the pit test! In this teaching, *pit* stands for *priesthood in training*. This is the place where Satan tries to strip you of your ministry or gifts and puts you in spiritual darkness, so you don't know how to get out. He's looking to keep you there as long as possible. Sadly, many Christians stay there for years; some, even their entire lifetime.

This is what the Bible says the Lord wants to do when we are thrown into a pit.

"He lifted me out of the slimy pit, out of the mud and mire; He set my feet on a rock and gave me a firm place to stand."
Psalm 40:2

Our bitterness, fear, anger, jealousy, or pain we have not dealt with can give the enemy a place to break into our life and keep us in a pit for a very long time. So, let's deal with our pain by forgiving others, getting healed from our wounds, and no longer giving the enemy ground to work with. Satan is just too happy to take that ground if we allow him to, through our un-healed pain.

A *pit* is really meant to show us what is within us that we don't see.

THE TEST OF BEING SOLD OUT

One of Joseph's brothers convinced the other brothers not to kill him but instead sell him into slavery in Egypt. Even then, we see the hand of God preserving his life. This is another test we all have to go through; the test of being sold out and re-jected.

Rejection not dealt with turns into rebellion; rebellion not dealt with turns into deception. Deception is a terrible place, as it causes us to believe something is truth, when it's not.

How do we receive deliverance from deception if we believe it to be true? By allowing the tests of life to bring us into ma-turity and away from rejection and rebellion. A lifestyle of rejection will lead to a root of bitterness, which the Word in Hebrews 12:15 says, defiles many. God wants to reveal within us His acceptance, love, and transformation right in the midst of this test. Walking out of the pain in our lives is a must if we desire to see the fulfillment of our destiny, calling, passions, or the dream we are carrying.

Through this test, the Lord teaches us to turn our rejection into His grace by blessing and loving people. Remember Jesus' teaching of 'The Beatitudes?' In Matthew 5:44, we are to show those same people who hurt us unmerited favor by forgiving them and by doing good to those who hate us and despitefully use us.

"But if you do not forgive others their sins, your Father won't forgive your sins."
Matthew 6:15

If we want our sins forgiven, we need to forgive others for theirs.

Walking in forgiveness is extremely crucial to passing all our tests, as the Bible gives us the answers to every test of life we find ourselves in. Another Kingdom principle that will transform our life is:

The Word of God contains transforming power to build our character in the midst of every test we find ourselves in.

That transformed character will begin to carry the weight of God's glory in our lives and ministry. Isaiah 55:11 says that His Word shall not return void, but will fulfill the purpose for which it was intended.

THE TEST OF TEMPTATION

Joseph had another major test to go through. This time, it was in Potiphar's home with Potiphar's wife who lusted after and desired him.

"One day he went into the house to attend to his duties, and none of the household servants were inside. She caught him by his cloak and said, 'Come to bed with me!' But he left his cloak in her hand and ran out of the house."
Genesis 39:11–12

Joseph walked in such honor and purity that he never thought of taking Potiphar's wife in that way. When temptation presented itself, Joseph didn't entertain it; he ran! Like Joseph, when the test of temptation to sin is at our door, we also need to run! Remember in Genesis 4:7, when God told Cain that sin was crouching at his door? Well, we know the outcome of that story. Cain didn't run from the temptation but gave into it and murdered his brother, Abel.

Grace teaches us to say, "No," to all ungodliness so don't entertain those thoughts. Sin always begins in the mind, where it is conceived. We need to deal with our issues and no longer yield to them

Let's continue Joseph's story, with more of our tests of life in the next chapter.

SECRET KINGDOM PRINCIPLES

Tests of life are the way of the King to
prepare us for our destiny.

Learn to be content in every circumstance we
find ourselves in – pleasant or difficult.

Learn to move beyond the pain in our life
in order to walk healed and whole.

There is no place for jealousy in the Kingdom of
God, if we want to walk in great authority.

A *pit* is really meant to show us what is
within us that we don't see.

Rejection not dealt with turns into rebellion; rebellion
not dealt with turns into deception. Deception
is a terrible place, as it causes us to believe
something is truth, when it's not.

If we want our sins forgiven, we need to
forgive others for theirs.

The Word of God contains transforming power to
build our character in the midst of every test
we find ourselves in.

Daniel 2:22 He reveals the deep and secret things...

Chapter 4

EXTRAORDINARY TIMES PART 2

"But we also rejoice in our sufferings, because we know that suffering produces perseverance; perseverance, character; and character, hope."
Romans 5:4 (BSB)

THE TEST OF FALSE ACCUSATION

After everything Joseph had been through since first being thrown into a pit by his jealous brothers, he made it to a palace. Life couldn't have been any better for him. That was until Potiphar's wife falsely accused Joseph of attempted rape just when he thought life wasn't going too badly.

"When his master heard the story his wife told him, saying, 'This is how your slave treated me,' he burned with anger. Joseph's master took him and put him in prison, the place where the king's prisoners were confined."
Genesis 39:19

We need to bless those who persecute us.

The test of false accusations can be very hard to deal with because it's natural for us to want to defend ourselves. What should our attitude be? Roman's 12:14 says, we need to bless those who persecute us. That's right, we are to bless not curse! Matthew 5:44 takes it even a step further, with the Lord instructing us to *love* our enemies and also pray for those who spitefully use us and persecute us.

There are blessings stored up for those who pass these tests. We are reminded again when Jesus was being nailed to the cross. He asked his Father to forgive those who were driving the nails in His hands and feet and those crying out for Him to be crucified. He also told his Father that they didn't know what they were doing. What a powerful example He gave us in how to respond to those who falsely accuse us, being that He was also falsely accused.

"Do not take revenge, my dear friends, but leave room for God's wrath, for it is written: 'It is mine to avenge; I will repay,' says the Lord.'"
Romans 12:19

In my earlier days, I had an experience which proved to be an invaluable lesson in my life. I overheard a co-worker telling a customer some wrong information and spoke up in an effort to help him. He was a new salesman, so I thought he would welcome the help. Instead, he accused me of trying to steal his customer which was not my intention at all. Still, he screamed at me, said some very mean things, and told me he would never talk to me again.

The whole incident caught me totally off guard, and I became extremely upset. When I went to the Lord about it, He told me to humble myself and go to my co-worker to ask his forgiveness. I reminded the Lord that I didn't do what the man had accused me of, but He reminded *me* of Romans 12:19, which said God would take care of circumstances on my behalf.

So, I humbled myself, apologized and asked my co-worker for forgiveness. Sadly, he said he would never forgive me and would not accept my apology. I thought to myself, "Well that sure didn't go as I expected," but felt I had obeyed what God asked me to do. This man proceeded to gossip about me to all my co-workers, continuing to accuse me of what he believed I had done to him. Still, I said nothing in return and within a short time, he was let go from the job.

God taught me, He would bring truth to light in His own time and not mine. I now understood that by blessing those who were persecuting me, it allowed God to come to my aid. If I had stood my ground, attempted to defend myself, and hadn't taken the low road, I am sure the outcome would have been quite different.

We may find ourselves in a *prison* or *situation* we don't feel we deserve, but how we respond while we are there will make all the difference in the world. It will also determine how long we need to be in that *prison – situation* in order to bring us into maturity. His ways are so contrary to our fleshly way of handling all these tests of life we go through. We need to allow *all* our tests to transform our lives, so we begin to actually *live* the Word of God and not only memorize or be able to quote those scriptures.

THE TEST OF BEING FORGOTTEN

In Genesis 40:22–23, Joseph interpreted a dream for Pharaoh's cupbearer and asked him to remember him when he got out of prison. However, the chief cupbearer did not remember Joseph and forgot all about him. Consequently, Joseph was in prison some additional years after asking the cupbearer to remember him.

Could it be possible that Joseph still hadn't quite learned to wait on the Lord's timing, as maybe he was trying to get out of prison before it was time? I can almost imagine the Lord, when hearing Joseph's request to the cupbearer, saying to Himself, "No, he's not quite ready to fulfill this huge destiny I have planned for him." Or possibly, "He's not mature enough to be given the keys to the car."

Have we ever tried to make something happen, and it didn't turn out well? I know I have!

So, another test we might face in life is being forgotten and cast aside. You know, that place where it feels like no one understands you, no one cares, people exclude you, or you're being passed over. We need to remember no matter what circumstance we find ourselves in – whether in the midst of a prison or cave experience – Hebrews 13:5 says, God will never leave or forsake us. We need to take comfort in that truth and trust Him to deliver us as He promises He will.

Why are these tests allowed? Sure, they bring feelings to the surface when we are not acknowledged, when we're passed over or when what we have desired is given to another. What is their real purpose in our life?

It is in our tests where we begin to fully understand who we truly are in Christ and that identity leads us into maturity.

When Joseph was left in prison and forgotten by the cup-bearer, he probably didn't understand, at that time, why he wasn't remembered. But even then, God was preparing him for the palace.

Please understand, unless we go *through* the process of passing these tests, we will not be mature enough to enter into that dream of destiny. Remember, we can't hurry the process, skip a step, or take a shortcut. In doing so, we just might be aborting the very thing God intends to promote us with! We never fail a test in the Kingdom but get to take them over and over again until we pass them. We just keep going around that same mountain, again and again.

For example, if there is a boss at work whom we have difficulty with, and we just can't stand it anymore, we may leave the job for another. Don't be surprised if we encounter that same type of person again. It may be a new job and they might go by a different name, but until we learn how to deal with that type of person, we're going to keep encountering them over and over again. Some people go from job to job never learning to pass that test – or even worse, from marriage to marriage.

I don't know about you, but I want to see what the Lord is doing in the midst of *all* my tests of life!

**If we can't pass our test, maybe it's time to find someone
to minister inner healing in that area.**

Recently, in my own life, the Lord put me into multiple circumstances which revealed how I felt people and God were passing me by. This had affected me very deeply! I am a firm believer in the inner healing ministry, so I met with someone to seek out the root of why I felt that way. The Lord led me back to my early childhood when we had a foster child in our home. She was very compliant, I wasn't, and always felt my mother favored her over me. The Lord led me back to a memory, when I was very young at Christmas, where I felt my mother had given the foster child a better Christmas present than she had given me. I also remembered how I became jealous, *feeling passed over.*

Jesus brought that memory to me and revealed how my present had actually cost so much more than hers. More importantly, He showed me the truth about how my mother felt about me, and how He felt about me. I forgave my mother and the foster child, broke that lie, and in turn, received a tremendous healing in my life. Now, when put into those very same circumstances – those which triggered feelings of hurt and jealousy – I no longer have feelings that God and man are passing me by, as they are gone and no longer cause me pain.

Since that healing moment, it seems as though the Lord has opened a spiritual door and thrust me further into destiny.

THOSE WHO SOW HONOR WILL…

In Genesis 41:12–14, Joseph is brought in to interpret Pharaoh's dream as the cupbearer *finally* remembered him. The Lord also gave him a strategic plan for the upcoming famine.

The truth is, in God's perfect timing, when everything within and without is prepared and ready, we will be remembered and given plans and strategies for the assignment we have been prepared for, just like Joseph.

> *"Then Pharaoh said to Joseph, 'Since God has made all this known to you, there is no one so discerning and wise as you. You shall be in charge of my palace, and all my people are to submit to your orders. Only with respect to the throne will I be greater than you."*
> Genesis 41:39–40

In this passage, we see the results that honoring those not worthy of our honor has in our life. Joseph walked a lifetime of honor toward others, even those who did him wrong. As we sow honor into others, we reap honor back into our lives from God. That is what I want for my life, to walk in such honor that releases me into an even greater destiny to impact lives and nations.

Allow our tests of life to make us better and not bitter!

As we've walked through Joseph's life, we see a picture of a more mature man who has walked through more pain and rejection than we may have had to deal with in our lifetime. Yet, he passed every test of life thrown at him, allowing them to make him better and not bitter. He became one who was now capable of ruling a nation as second in command to Pharaoh. He was one who God could now trust with *'the keys to the car'* because He knew Joseph wouldn't hurt himself or others, but would walk in love and humility before God and man. There was no more haughtily flaunting his coat before others or tattling. He had obtained wisdom to know when to share the dreams God had given him, whom to share them with, and who not to share them with. More importantly, he also knew when not to share them at all! Joseph grew in the Lord, the things of the Kingdom, learned Kingdom secrets his tests of life had taught him, and so much more.

When this happens in our own lives, we can be in *prison* one day and in the *palace* the next – SUDDENLY! Just as Joseph did, we will be able to look back on our lives and see the hand of God working to transform us for a destiny way beyond our comprehension.

Do you think Joseph could have ever imagined what was in store for his life when he had those dreams he didn't understand so many years before?

Let's continue with Joseph's story.

THE LORD IN OUR TESTS

His brothers were sent to Egypt by their father Jacob to find grain during the food famine. When the brothers arrived at the palace, they bowed before him, not recognizing who he was. Little did they know they were fulfilling the dream Joseph had shared with them some twenty years earlier, when he was just a teenager. The dream was that *their* wheat sheaves were bowing down to *his*, and here they were bowing down to him, asking for wheat.

Eventually, Joseph revealed his true identity to them. I'm sure no one was more surprised – and stunned – than his brothers were at that moment. Now watch what Joseph tells them next.

> *"But don't be upset, and don't be angry with yourselves for selling me to this place. It was God who sent me here ahead of you to preserve your lives."*
> Genesis 45:5–8

Wait a minute! Weren't *these* those same brothers who hated him and sold him into slavery in the first place? Yes, these were the same ones! What was even more amazing was that Joseph had compassion on them, to the point he didn't want them to be hard or angry with themselves for what they had done to him. Instead, Joseph, without an ounce of vengeance, told them it was actually God who sent him there – for their own benefit!

Wow! That is true forgiveness and maturity at the highest level – the level of Christ's forgiveness!

We find here in Scripture, it was all part of God's master plan.

Everything from being ridiculed, stripped of his prized family heirloom, hated and despised, rejected, abandoned in a pit and left for dead, sold into slavery by those he trusted, falsely accused, lied about, thrown into prison, forgotten – all of it. Every test he faced, every trial he endured, every personal attack was in the Master's grand blueprint for destiny and greatness.

God is *not* the author of bad things happening in our lives, but sin and Satan are. God foreknew what would happen to Joseph and used all the awful things that happened in his life for good; just as He does in our life!

"And we know that in all things God works for the good of those
who love Him, who have been called according to His purpose."
Romans 8:28

These events were very instrumental in order to accomplish two very important things. First, it was to change the character of Joseph and bring him to the place of growth and maturity needed to prepare him to rule and reign as second in command to Pharaoh. We are actually being prepared by *our* tests of life to rule and reign in the destiny God has prepared just for us! Secondly, Joseph was being used to preserve the entire nation of Israel during a time of devastating famine.

"He sent a man before them – Joseph – who was sold as a slave.
They hurt his feet with fetters. He was laid in irons. Until
the time that his word came to pass, the Word
of the LORD tested him."
Psalm 105:17–19

Do you see that? From the very time of Joseph's word (his dreams) until the time they came to pass in his life, *"the Word of the Lord tested him."* So, another secret is:

Until the time His Word comes to pass for us, the Word of the Lord tests us.

How many times do we go through tests of life and actually recognize them as tests from the Lord? It's time we *change* the way we are looking at them and begin to allow the Lord to do whatever is needed in us, knowing that every one of them is preparing us for the great destiny God planned for our life. It's time to seek the Lord on how to line our lives up with the Word of God and do what He says to do.

Throughout all these tests, the most important key to passing them is walking in a lifestyle of forgiveness. Unforgiveness and bitterness are the greatest hindrances to being released into our destiny.

Joseph had forgiven his brothers for what they did to him because he *understood* that *all* these tests made him who he was and how they were used to launch him into this great destiny. Joseph chose to walk out of his pain! We can choose not to stay in our pain, by forgiving others and allowing the Lord to heal us.

Joseph was being trained his entire lifetime, for he had a lifetime gift of governing everywhere he was – at home, Potiphar's house, and in prison. All this prepared him to rule in the palace, and *all* his tests brought him into the *maturity* needed to become a great leader.

After seeing this, I asked the Lord to show me my lifetime gift, and He did. I'm sure if we ask Him what ours is, we will see something in our life that is a pattern that happens *everywhere* we go, which will be a key to what we are being prepared for in our palace! In this book, the palace represents ruling and reigning in the assignment the Lord has been preparing us for. Rest assured, even though we may not understand it now, we *are* being prepared for that dream God has in His heart for us!

THE TEST OF HUMILITY

There is a *final* test in Joseph's life we must all pass, which is the test of what we become when we reach that dream we have or that prophetic word spoken over us. If we passed all the previous tests of life and learned all God intended us to, we will be in a better position to pass this next test; the humility test.

We need to be healed and delivered in every area of our life where the enemy can gain a foothold and cause us to fall. If we get to the palace where we are realizing our dream and walking in it, but still have unhealed, unresolved, or broken areas in our life, then we may fail the test and fall into pride – *all while living the dream.*

There are believers and ministry leaders who started well, but later in life fell into deception and didn't finish well. Even when we look at these men and women who were great people of faith, we can learn from both their successes and failures. We should honor them for what they brought to the Body of Christ and not discount their entire life because they didn't finish well.

I encourage us to listen to those who love us. When they

speak to us about something that needs to be changed, don't get defensive just because we don't see it ourselves. If we hear the same thing from several people, it's probably a blind spot we are not able to see in ourselves.

Find an inner healing ministry and allow the Lord to heal those broken places in our life, so our responses or traits will be transformed. There are reasons why we respond in wrong ways and inner healing follows that fruit in our life back to the root of why we do the things we do. Jesus heals and replaces all our lies, with His truth to make us free, so that our behavior and responses are transformed.

We need to walk as unoffended lovers and offer forgiveness to those who have hurt us, just like Joseph did with his brothers. I believe if we have to keep taking a test over and over, it may be time to follow the fruit to the root to get it healed.

From that place of healing, promotion comes, character is transformed, and we get closer to that place of maturity. More importantly, our wrong attitudes and behaviors change, and we can walk further into expressing the love of the Father to others.

When we learn the truths that come from passing the tests we face and seeing the value they have in our life, we will be able to walk in perfect peace in the midst of all of life's storms. We will be able to say, like the apostle Paul in Philippians 4:11: *"I have learned the secret of being content, whatever the circumstances."*

If we truly understand what these trials are accomplishing in our life, then it will be easy to obey this verse in James 1:2–4, to consider it pure joy when we face every type of trial. Not joyful about the circumstance, but joy in knowing our trials are producing maturity, so that we will lack nothing.

Joseph was pretty happy and content governing the family at home and probably would have *settled* for doing just that the rest of his life, but God had a *greater* plan for Joseph, a destiny he would've never imagined for himself.

When we find ourselves in places we don't like and think we should be somewhere else in life, sometimes we fail to realize the Lord has a greater destiny than we could ever imagine for us. He knows when we are not ready, and would settle for a lot less than our divine destiny if left to ourselves.

There is an assignment in the heart of God for *us*, just as He had for Joseph; it's a dream greater than we could ever imagine!

So don't settle for less than the biggest dream you have for your life. It may be a dream you don't yet understand but is greater than anything you could imagine.

Every *answer* to every test is found in the Word of God.

Make it our goal to pass every test we find ourselves in. Look for the answers in the Word of God to understand how to think and respond in all our tests of life. Every *answer* to every test is found in the Word of God, so allow our mind and heart to be transformed in the midst of our tests. Then, when God knows we are ready, the doors of destiny will open to *us*; and we will walk into the greatest assignments of our life.

Remember, *all* our tests are meant to produce spiritual growth to become mature sons of God. This secret changed the way I looked at my trials, as I now understood the reason for them and began to cooperate with the Spirit *in* them. This revolutionized my life!

Lord, I declare lightbulbs are going off in the minds of those who begin to see their own circumstances through the life of Joseph. They are those who will pass every test of life they find themselves in, and be thrust into the great assignments which You have planned for them. I also declare destiny will overtake them! In Jesus' name, Amen.

SECRET KINGDOM PRINCIPLES

We need to bless those who persecute us.

It is in our tests where we begin to fully understand who we truly are in Christ and that identity leads us into maturity.

If we can't pass our test, maybe it's time to find
someone to minister inner healing in that area.

Allow our tests of life to make us better
and not bitter!

Until the time His Word comes to pass for
us, the Word of the Lord tests us.

There is an assignment in the heart of God for *us*,
just as He had for Joseph; it's a dream
greater than we could ever imagine!

Every *answer* to every test is found
in the Word of God.

Chapter 5

BACK SEAT TO PROMOTION

"But when you are invited, take the lowest place, so that when your host comes, he will say to you, 'Friend, move up to a better place.' Then you will be honored in the presence of all the other guests."
Luke 14:10

Jesus revealed another secret of the Kingdom in the parable He spoke about in the book of Luke. Personally, this Kingdom secret caused another shift in the way I looked at attaining a platform or position in the Kingdom of God. People may look for a platform to operate in their gifts and calling, but the Lord has something to say about this in a parable He taught.

Many people were invited to a dinner at the home of a local Pharisee. When Jesus noticed the invited guests vying to sit at the seats of honor at the head of the table, He began to teach them using a parable about guests attending a wedding feast. He told them when they were invited somewhere, not to sit in the seats of honor because when someone more important came in, the host may ask them to move. Not only would they have to move, but would also be embarrassed by this request, as everyone would see what had transpired.

Jesus gave us a better way:

"For those who exalt themselves will be humbled and those who humble themselves will be exalted."
Luke 14:11

Jesus told us in this parable that a better way would be to take a seat at the lowest part of the table and wait for the host to come and tell us he has a better seat for us. Then we will be honored in front of others instead of embarrassed. Here is the secret:

If we exalt ourselves, we will be humbled; if we humble ourselves, we will be exalted.

Some years ago, I was struggling with seeing other people being esteemed higher and given more attention than I was. I dealt with feeling overlooked, not only as a person but also for who I was in the Kingdom and what I carried. At the time, I knew I should be okay with everything; however, my emotions got the worst of me, and I became offended. When I read this passage, particularly verse 10 where Jesus says, *"When invited, take the last place or seat,"* this really ministered to me.

I knew the Lord wanted to teach me this truth and also that

His love and acceptance should've been enough for me. It was a very hard place to be because I also knew I had a great prophetic destiny, yet it seemed to be nowhere in sight. I found myself wanting man's acceptance and approval to be given a place.

I came to understand how our flesh loves the seats of honor, but true promotion comes from the Lord. I needed to learn how to take a seat at the foot of the table, but didn't realize this lesson would come in such a literal way. Not long after the Lord began dealing with me about this, I went on a mission trip with a group of people. It gave me the perfect opportunity to really live this out.

Every evening at dinnertime, long tables were pushed together. The leaders would sit at one end of the table, and everyone else would fill in. As others took their places near the head of the table, I purposely chose the foot of the table. Understanding the Lord was dealing with me, I intentionally sat the furthest away from the seats considered the honor end of the table. The entire time, I kept saying to the Lord, "You have to be enough!"

On the last night of our ministry trip, I once again took the seat at the foot of the table where the young children, of the leader of that country's ministry, were seated. Their mother told me I should move to be able to converse with the adults, but I told her that I was good where I was. To my utter surprise, the ministry leader moved his children over and sat directly across from me. I had his undivided attention the entire night because his children were between us and the rest of the group.

I was reminded of verse 11 and had humbled myself by

85

choosing the last seat every night, and the Lord exalted me with a seat of honor to teach me the truth of this parable. That very evening, I learned first–hand, another secret of the Kingdom.

Wait for the Lord's promotion, for He will promote us in His perfect time and season.

The Lord was trying to help me understand that if I would learn to take the back seat, He would see to it I was given a seat of honor at just the right time. I learned from this experience, how to wait for the Lord to promote me to the next level, and not try to promote myself. Promotion truly comes from the Lord!

In this next season, there are those who will be GIVEN great authority, those who have learned the secret of knowing how to come under authority. They will know how to serve, to be last, to wait for God to open doors, and to stay hidden. They will also understand how to not serve their own vision, dream, and calling first and foremost, but instead serve others and wait for God's promotion to come. These are those who are earmarked to be truly great in the Kingdom; those who walk in a culture of honor and love, as Jesus did. Matthew 20:28 says, Jesus didn't come to be served, but to serve.

We need to ask the Lord to show us how to walk in Kingdom principles. He is looking for those who will allow these principles to transform their lives; who are willing to pay the price for these secrets, so He can pour His glory into them. He wants this emerging apostolic Church to become what He intends. In

1 John 4:17 it says of Jesus, *"As He is, so are we in this world."* It's time to look like Jesus, think, speak, act, and do what He did here on the earth. It's also time to walk in the greater works He promised we would do.

The Lord wants us to not only be people who walk in His likeness but also in all of His Word, and not just in the verses that don't require sacrifice. Jesus, according to Hebrews 5:8, was our example of the ultimate sacrifice and learned obedience by the things *He* suffered. So, we also need to allow the things *we* suffer to bring us into obedience to the Word of God.

PROMOTION COMES FROM GOD

You remember the Lord spoke to me about attending a new church and learning about the *new wine*? The senior leaders were in the process of moving from a pastor–centered culture to an apostolic one. I was thankful to be able to see this transition of moving from the old wine of tradition into the new wine of biblical church government.

I am grateful for the new wine they modeled to help me understand how these roles were transitioning. Today, he is no longer the pastor but senior leader and apostolic covering of the church, as well as in so many lives aligned with that ministry. He travels the globe speaking at conferences, schools of ministry, to business leaders, and government officials. His wife, also a senior leader with him, leads her own benevolence ministry, has a school of supernatural ministry, and speaks worldwide. While he travels, there is a pastor–teacher in the pulpit. While attending this church, I heard the Lord speak to me another secret:

"Serve the apostle's vision, and he will serve yours."

I knew the Lord was talking to me about the leader of our church. The motive of my heart was not to serve with an ulterior motive to have him serve my vision but serve his vision and as I had learned, wait for the Lord to promote mine. I went to him and told him what the Lord said to me and asked him how I might serve his vision. He asked me to head up the registration tables at the conferences and man their product/book table after Church on Sundays. Even though I was leading a group of apostles and prophets in my own ministry, I served his vision in the church with joy, taking the back seat and waiting to be invited to a seat in the front.

After a year of this type of serving, my leaders asked me to teach a series called, *The Glory School,* which were classes that taught people how to walk in the supernatural realm. I didn't feel led to teach this and declined, but several months later they told me the Lord impressed them that I was supposed to teach this class. When I went before the Lord, He said, "I don't always speak to you directly about what I would have you do, but I also speak to the leaders on your behalf." I taught the school and anything else they asked me to do after that. Teaching not only in the church but also at a home group meeting. These times of teaching became the greatest blessing! From this season, I came to recognize the teaching call on my life and saw it flourish under the leadership of that church. I also learned during that time how to submit, honor, and wait for the Lord to promote me.

I don't think we understand how truly important being in

right relationship with authority is in the Kingdom. Just look at the right relationship found in the Godhead – Father, Son, and Holy Spirit and we will begin to get a glimpse of how God sees authority and submission. We need to begin to understand how truly important this is. Imagine having no divine order in the Godhead and what that would look like. Yikes! We *really* need to grab hold of this truth.

I submitted myself to serve an apostle and waited on God for His promotion. It says in Psalm 127:1, *"Unless the Lord builds the house, they labor in vain."* Too many are trying to build the house themselves, not comprehending their labor is in vain. There is a better way!

Right in the midst of being *very* happy in my church and ministry, I heard the Lord speak to me to move to another state. With my husband's full support and agreement, we moved from the north to the south. In an eighty–day real estate market, our home sold the first day for more than asking price. When God calls you to do something, He prepares the way, as well as every detail surrounding that call.

FROM HEAVEN TO EARTH

The Lord led us to a new church where the senior leaders also had a heart to see the church transition from a pastor–centered church to an apostolic one with the five–fold ministry in place. They are open to everything it will take to make this transition and the Spirit of God is moving among us, preparing and putting things into place.

Shortly after I started attending there, I was asked to teach on the five–fold ministry. Since that subject is near and dear to my heart, I agreed. In preparing for this teaching, the Lord began to shift my understanding even further. He revealed deeper Kingdom *secrets* I never understood before about divine order from heaven to earth. The Lord always does things with patterns and numbers in the Bible, and this is *significant* for our understanding of the Kingdom of God.

While preparing for this teaching, I received a revelation on the pattern of *three* in the Bible. I researched the significance of this number and found; "Biblically, the number three represents divine wholeness, completeness and perfection." (*www.kansascity.com/living/religion/article1319649.html*)

I am sharing what the Lord showed me that night. We know there are three parts of God: Father, Jesus (Son), and Holy Spirit. They are the same being but have three different functions. They are all equally God, but model a divine order for us to understand how it should look on earth as it is in heaven, or heaven to earth in this case.

The Father leads, Jesus submits to the Father and only does what He sees and hears the Father doing, and the Holy Spirit teaches, comforts, and points people to Jesus. *They* model for us the government of heaven *we* need to bring to earth.

There is complete *unity* between the three, as well as *honoring, loving,* and *esteeming* one another. Each one understands Their role, function, and who They are in the Godhead. They also know what they each are responsible for and depend on one another to fulfill Their roles. It works so beautifully, and love is at the core of all They do. They make up a government of three in heaven and the Kingdom of God. All of heaven submits to this order and *all* the heavenly beings under this government flourish.

We are called to bring heaven to earth, and this is the model we see in the government of heaven that we need to bring to earth. Jesus taught us to pray in Matthew 6:10, *"Thy will be done, on earth as it is in heaven."*

Here is another secret:

In the government of God, He has appointed, first apostles, second prophets, and third teachers – following the Kingdom pattern in heaven for divine order in the Church.

> *"And God has appointed in the church, first apostles, second prophets, third teachers, then miracles, then gifts of healing, helping, administrating, and various kinds of tongues."*
> I Corinthians 12:28 (ESV)

What the Spirit revealed was that God laid out in this verse the *divine order* of Church government with apostles being first, prophets being second, and teachers being third. I saw in this verse the *same* pattern of three repeated in the Church that was patterned after the heavenly, and how each position on the earth follows the pattern of three in heaven.

Please hear me in giving these analogies; I am talking functionally and not literally. I'm saying there are *principles* of divine order in the Godhead which we need to understand *in order* to bring that pattern of three from heaven to earth.

Here is what I received from the Lord that night: The apostle is 'likened' to God, being the leader of the church or ministry they are called to. The prophet is 'likened' to Jesus who only says what He hears the Father saying. The teacher is 'likened' to the Holy Spirit who teaches us all things and also points us to Jesus by their teaching. What a revelation that was to me!

All other positions fall under these three governmental roles in the Church. I received a glimpse of the pattern of divine Church government while meditating on this verse. I realized we needed to bring this pattern of three from the *heavenly* government to the *earthly* in order for the church to operate in unity, love, peace, harmony, submission, power, and glory. We desperately need to return to God's original design manifested in heaven, once again on the earth.

The apostle, prophet, and teacher need to realize they are also equal like the Godhead is, but in the Body of Christ they *too* have different functions. They are equal, but each has a divine order for the Church to function governmentally on earth, as God intended. In walking in unity, they honor, love, and esteem one another just as the Godhead models in the heavenly government. This heavenly model allows us to understand what each role is responsible for, and how to depend on one another to fulfill each of the roles. When this happens, everyone in the Church will *flourish* just as they do in the heavenly government.

The apostle receives a vision for the work God has called them to. They are given great authority and government of the Kingdom to accomplish what the Lord has given them for that vision. Heaven grants them the sphere of authority, mantle, and heavenly blueprints given for their assignments.

The apostle is in the lead, just as God is in the heavenly model. They have a father's heart, receive divine strategies for that vision, train people, empower them into ministries, and set into place those called into the five–fold giftings. They are also given to prayer, teach the Word, establish new works as builders, and walk in signs and wonders. The apostle receives prophetic words from the prophet and is given the strategy, timing, and government for that word. Apostles are honored as servant leaders, walk in great authority, and are visionaries.

The prophet is to hear from God, just as Jesus did, and only speaks what the Father is saying; to bring clarity to the Church, region, and individual lives. They work closely under the leadership of the apostle, just as Jesus did with the Father. Prophets release people into their destinies by the prophetic word, give warnings, hear direction for the church and region, work closely with, and also speak into the vision given to the apostle. They train other prophets, walk in signs and wonders, and are honored for hearing from God and telling us things from heaven. The Word says in Amos 3:7:

> *"Surely the Sovereign Lord does nothing without revealing His plan to His servants the prophets."*

This verse is what sets the prophet of the five-fold ministry gift apart from those who prophesy, which is something we are *all* able to do. There is a remarkable difference between the two, as the purpose for one who prophesies is found in:

> *"But the one who prophecies (all of us) speaks to people for their strengthening, encouragement, and comfort."*
> I Corinthians 14:3

So, the distinction between those who prophesy and the prophet, is that the prophet prophesies as we all do, but also hears what the plans of God are before they come to pass; gives warnings of things to come; hears direction for the Church, region, or globally; trains other prophets; and supports the apostle's vision.

I see people who prophesy in Church pretty regularly and are called prophets, even though they have not been appointed to the five–fold ministry of prophet. They actually strengthen, encourage, and comfort people, according to I Corinthians 14:3.

We read about a New Testament prophet, Agabus, who prophesies a famine is coming in Acts 11:28, and warns the apostle Paul what will happen to him when going to Jerusalem.

> *"After we had been there several days, a prophet named*
> *Agabus came down from Judea. Coming over to us, he*
> *took Paul's belt, tied his own hands and feet with it and*
> *said, 'The Holy Spirit says, In this way, the Jewish leaders*
> *in Jerusalem will bind the owner of this belt and*
> *will hand him over to the Gentiles.'"*
> Acts 21:10–11

The five–fold teacher gifting is given to bring truth and understanding to the Body of Christ from the Word of God. Teachers receive supernatural revelation, accompanied by the power and authority that transforms lives, to bring people into spiritual growth and maturity for the destiny each one has been given. Teachers speak truth to dispel error and lead people out of deception through the *revelatory* teaching from the Word of God. They are also under the leadership of the apostle and honored for bringing revelation, truth, correction, and transformation into the Body of Christ.

The prophet and teacher are under the leadership of the

apostle, *exactly* the same way Jesus and the Holy Spirit are under the leadership of God. They are equal, but different! Remember, in observing the heavenly model, we can understand the earthly.

In the book of Acts, these are the three sent out to establish new works and churches. The apostle and prophet were sent first and then those who were gifted teachers followed, to bring the new believers into maturity.

> *"All are not apostles, are they? All are not prophets, are they? All are not teachers, are they?"*
> I Corinthians 12:29 (NASB)

We see from this verse that we are not *all* apostles, prophets, or teachers. Those whom God has called, appointed, and anointed for these positions, are those who are earmarked to walk in the five–fold ministry. But, we can *all* prophesy!

According to I Corinthians 12:28, these are the *three* governmental positons we see set forth in the New Testament, with the remaining two five–fold ministries also given to equip the Church and bring them into maturity.

Evangelists are empowered to preach the Gospel and bring *multitudes* into the Kingdom of God. They walk in great signs and wonders, and prophecy, as Jesus did when He evangelized Israel. They are submitted to the leadership of the apostle and are honored for the harvest they are gathering.

Pastors are needed in *every* church to minister the Father's heart to His Bride. They walk in deep compassion and come alongside those needing a shepherd. They counsel, exhort, build people up, and are in submission to the leadership of the apostle. They are honored for what they do to build the Body of Christ.

All these five–fold ministry gifts are evidenced within Jesus and if we want to know what these *really* look like, we can study His life. HE is our example and displays the character and love each of the five–fold members should have for one another and the Body of Christ.

Every member of the five–fold ministry team should esteem, honor, and serve one another. What a beautiful picture we see demonstrated in the Godhead, where God honors Jesus, but Jesus is submitting to and serving the Father, with the Holy Spirit also in submission. All three model the servant leadership we need to walk in and paint an awesome picture for us of the newly transitioned Church. We must return back to God's original design of Church government established in the Word of God, once again bringing New Testament divine order from heaven to earth.

This type of divine order will usher us into becoming the *Bride* the world is longing to see without spot or blemish, we see in Ephesians 5:27. We will be full of unconditional love, serving one another in the fear of the Lord, and will finally become the mature sons of God the earth is groaning for in Romans 8:19. This will be a place where there is neither male nor female, but where we will begin to look at one another after the Spirit. We will truly esteem the calling and place each one has been given in the Body of Christ.

We need to begin looking at one another's calling and realize not one of us is better or higher, only different. In Ephesians 2:20, the apostle and prophet are actually at the bottom as the foundation that all the others are built upon. The rest of the

Body should be esteeming and honoring the apostle and prophet as their *servant* leaders. All of us should, as Ephesians 5:21 says, submit one to another out of reverence to Christ.

We should never respond as someone who is 'lording our position over another,' as there is neither a model or place for 'lording' in the Kingdom of God! 'Lording over' means: *'To behave as if one is in control of; to make a display of having an advantage over or superiority to.'*

Instead, according to Romans 12:3, we should not think more highly of ourselves. Philippians 2:3 tells us to do nothing out of selfish ambition but in *humility*, to esteem others more highly than ourselves. The Bible is quite clear on how we are to respond in Galatians 5:13; to not use our freedom to indulge our flesh, but humbly serve one another in love.

The Lord spoke to me some years ago and said, "In the days to come, many will walk in My power, but only those who walk in My character will be carriers of My glory."

Many will walk in God's power, but only those who walk in His character will be carriers of His glory.

When we begin to operate in these divine, biblical precepts, the glory of the Lord will be such an integral part of the Church. Signs and wonders will be commonplace and thousands upon thousands will flock to the Lord. For they will be drawn by the Love of God flowing through us and by the love we have for one another. Love and Honor will be the catalyst that draws them to Jesus!

When we model this 'on earth as it is in heaven' government, we will walk with no more offenses, discord, separations, judgments, criticism, hatred, unforgiveness, and bitterness that we see plaguing the Church today. All of *that* would be replaced with love, honor, respect, obedience, unity, submission, peace, joy, and all the Fruit of the Spirit. What a glorious church that will be! We *will* become that Bride without spot or blemish...

**We need to *first* understand the heavenly pattern of
divine order, to understand the earthly –
in order to bring heaven to earth!**

We also see the *same* pattern of three modeled in the home with Jesus being the head of the husband and the husband being the head of the wife. Jesus is the *model* that helps us understand how that headship should be demonstrated between husband and wife, as Ephesians 5:25 says that husbands are to love their wives as Christ loves the Church. Again, there is no place for 'lording over' *anyone* in the Body of Christ as Jesus never did and is our model, sacrificing Himself for us.

Remember, these are not literal but *functional* principles to help us understand the heavenly pattern of three in order to bring heavenly divine order to earth in our homes.

With Jesus, in this home's pattern of three, 'likened' to the Heavenly Father in being the *leader*. The husband is 'likened' to Jesus where the husband *only* speaks to his wife and children what the Father is saying. The wife is 'likened' to the Holy Spirit who comforts and teaches as this is the mother's nature within her. Home will be a place where they also realize the husband and wife are equal, but have different functions. How different our homes would be if we really understood and walked in this heavenly divine order of loving and esteeming one another, as each one walks in their divine role in the home.

The husband would love his wife as Christ does the Church and would sacrifice himself for her, as Jesus did. He would only speak to his wife and children what he heard Jesus saying. God is love and it says in John 14:9 that if we see Jesus, we see the Father. So, love would be reigning in that home with the husband *demonstrating* the love of Christ to his family.

Wives would easily submit to and respect a man who acted like Jesus, and the wife would have the backing of heaven, as well as her husband, to teach and comfort the children. She would also walk alongside her husband and he would *depend* on her counsel, advice, and perspective, from the portion of God's attributes He planted within *her*. The husband would trust the wife's discernment and wisdom, given to her by God, as decisions are made together.

Mark 10:8 tells us that man and woman become one flesh when married. *One* of the ways we were designed to display that oneness in the home is by walking in dominion. Remember, only *together* do we display the full image of God's attributes as He originally designed us to flow with one another. We would become loving, healthy, and secure homes walking in divine order, in the *same* way that Jesus and the Holy Spirit walk in divine order and flow with one another.

The good news is that God is a redeemer of time. This is possible no matter how long we have been married or how far from this we have deviated. God is the God of the impossible and a miracle maker!

We now understand the pattern of three, modeled in the Kingdom government in heaven, the Church, and the home. It's time to bring the government of the Kingdom down from heaven to the earth once again. We *desperately* need to return to God's original design!

> *"A voice of one calling: 'In the wilderness prepare the way for the LORD; make straight in the desert a highway for our God.'"*
> Isaiah 40:3

I want to return all the way back to the beginning of my journey, when I said to the Lord, "Why are you showing me this? What can I do about it?" Here we are seventeen years later! I have been given a voice and revelation I didn't understand when God first gave me those verses regarding the five–fold ministry. This is one of the primary calls to write this book, to be *a voice crying in the wilderness to prepare the way* for the *reformation* of church government, as well as in teaching secret Kingdom principles.

In this restored government of God, EVERYONE will be doing the works of the ministry with some ministering to those inside the Church and the rest ministering to those outside the Church. In this season, many will be added to the Church and raised up to do the works of the ministry. For those who have an ear to hear what the Spirit is saying, they will be returning to divine order. There will be no more just sitting in the pews wanting to be fed, inspired, and doing no more than that! Each one will be pouring out of their lives to others in the assignments they are called to.

The purpose of the five–fold ministry is to train and equip *everyone* to be ministers of the Gospel. This is what will happen when we return to heavenly divine order to restore power and authority to operate as *one* again.

This is the passion of my heart and has been more than a seventeen year journey. I am waiting with great anticipation for the day we fully embrace the Word of God and become the Ecclesia the Lord intended us to be. I am confident the Lord is bringing these changes to those who have an ear to hear what the Spirit is speaking.

Again, sadly there will be those who will not want to change and will stay where the Church has been since Constantine brought in those changes. Remember, it's extremely difficult to break out of 1,700 years of traditions, but God has used reformers in every new season of the Church. The question is: Will we be one of them?

A true reformer walks in love and honor, even to those who resist and persecute them.

A reformer walks in love and honor; even to those who resist and persecute those who want to see this type of reformation. They will love those in opposition and keep their hearts and minds pure before God. Reformers do not oppose those who oppose them but walk in reformation, right in the midst of persecution. This reminds me of how they lived in the days of the New Testament.

Lord, I declare that those who have an ear to hear what the Spirit is saying will see and understand the Kingdom of God, the heavenly pattern of three, and His divine government from heaven to earth. They will return to God's original design in the church, home, and everywhere they find themselves; becoming loving reformers. In Jesus' name, Amen.

SECRET KINGDOM PRINCIPLES

If we exalt ourselves, we will be humbled; if we humble ourselves, we will be exalted.

Wait for the Lord's promotion, for He will promote us in His perfect time and season.

"Serve the apostle's vision, and he will serve yours."

In the government of God, He has appointed, first apostles, second prophets, and third teachers – following the Kingdom pattern in heaven for divine order in the Church.

Many will walk in God's power, but only those who walk in His character will be carriers of His glory.

We need to *first* understand the heavenly pattern of divine order, to understand the earthly – in order to bring heaven to earth!

A true reformer walks in love and honor, even to those who resist and persecute them.

Chapter 6

WHAT IT LOOKS LIKE

*"Be devoted to one another in brotherly love; give
preference to one another in honor."*
Romans 12:10 (NASB)

HONOR IS AN ACTION

We need to truly understand the utmost importance that honor holds in the Kingdom because it is so *essential* in this season, and *powerfully* opens heaven to us. We saw in the Life of David, the place of honor he held King Saul in. The more he honored Saul, the more the Lord honored David, so much that David was known as a man after God's own heart and was called a friend of God.

As *we* humble ourselves to honor those in authority over us – those we deem both worthy and *unworthy* of that honor – God exalts us. It's such a simple truth that is missing from the Church but one that will unlock the glory of God expressed through us to the world.

Another attribute that needs to be restored to the Church is loyalty to those God has called us to serve under. David was loyal to Saul, even while Saul was trying to murder him. David was so loyal to Saul in 2 Samuel 1:14–16, that he had the man who helped Saul die put to death for his involvement. David asked him, *"Why weren't you afraid to lift your hand to destroy the LORD's anointed?"* Consider this question in light of the fact that Saul was pursuing David for years to murder him. How many times do we lift our hands, by our words, to destroy God's anointed?

2 Samuel 9:1 says that after Saul died, David sent his servants to find the remainder of Saul's family, so he could show kindness to them. Do we see this kind of loyalty in the Church today? As soon as there's something we see or hear we don't like or agree with, so many of us are out of there! The definition of loyalty is: *'having or showing complete and constant support for someone or something.'*

Just like David, we need to become faithful to those leaders we deem to be unworthy of our loyalty; the Saul's in our life! Loyalty needs to be restored in the Church, so let it begin with us!

The kind of loyalty and faithfulness that David had for Saul needs to be established in our life.

If I hadn't learned to honor those leaders in my life who I thought of as unworthy of honor, I wouldn't be writing this book. It also wasn't until learning to honor difficult leaders that I was put into a church where honor was modeled and lived out by the leaders. They honored with such a depth of love and in a way I had not seen expressed before. I came into that church knowing how to honor, but to my joy, those new leaders were worthy of that honor. So another secret is.

The culture of the Kingdom is built upon honor; and is essential for us, to unlock government and power in the Kingdom of God.

This is a key to walking in the supernatural realm. The alternative is to be like the Corinthian church; where they had major trouble with Godly character, walked in carnal ways, but were highly gifted. Paul brought correction to them more than any other church.

Honor is multi–faceted, and love is so intertwined with honor that we can't walk in honor without it. Honor unlocks heaven, and heaven will supernaturally back those who have learned how to honor individuals who don't seem worthy of honor.

"Jesus said, 'If you love those who love you, what credit it that? For even sinners love those who love them.'"
Luke 6:32

We can also say, "If you honor those who honor you, what credit is that to you? For even sinners honor those who honor them," for honor is found in love. Heaven is looking for those who walk in such honor, to promote them with *greater* authority to transform everywhere they place their feet.

Remember the bible stories of David with Saul and Esther with Haman? David and Esther honored dishonorable authorities over them, and heaven moved supernaturally in both cases. After they honored those over them, David was raised to be a King after God's own heart and Esther to save a nation. Another secret is:

Honor releases heaven for supernatural miracles on our behalf.

Honor can save *us* like it did for David and Esther. Think of honor as one of those attributes that releases Heaven's authority to follow us, back us up, and work on our behalf no matter where we go.

Honor unlocks the gifts in others for impartation into *our* life.

Matthew 10:41 tells us when we receive a prophet in the name of a prophet, we also receive a prophet's reward. This means if we receive or honor that prophet as a true prophet, then the reward of what they carry is released; a prophetic word for us. In honoring one of my leaders for the government and authority he carried, government and authority were granted to me by heaven. This is a principle that always works through honor.

Let's look at other facets concerning honor and love that Jesus taught the multitudes and His own disciples. Walking in these ways will transform *our* life and every life around us, changing atmospheres wherever we go.

Take a moment and think about someone we have a difficult relationship with – possibly a family member, someone at work, church, or in our neighborhood – whom we struggle with. We are going to need that name for this next portion below.

Take a few moments and think about this person in light of what honor actually means. Read these characteristics and ask ourselves these questions, "Is honor increasing for them in my life? Are these honoring attributes expressed through me as I relate to that difficult person I thought of?"

Here are some definitions and synonyms for honor:

As a noun: *'high respect, esteem.'*

Synonyms: *'distinction, recognition, privilege, glory, kudos, prestige, merit, credit, importance, notability, respect, esteem.'*

As a verb: *'regard with great respect.'*

Synonyms: *'esteem, respect, admire, defer to, look up to, appreciate, value, adore.'*

The definition of what love looks like is found in I Corinthians 13:4–8. Let's see how our love measures up for that person we thought of:

> *"Love suffers long and is kind, does not envy, does not draw attention to itself or is puffed up, does not behave rudely, does not seek its own, is not provoked, thinks no evil, does not rejoice in iniquity, but rejoices with the truth, bears all things, believes all things, hopes all things, endures all things, LOVE NEVER FAILS!"*

According to this definition of love, how does our love measure up for that difficult person we are in relationship with? If we keep doing the things we have always done, we will keep getting the things we have always gotten. Let's change how we look at and respond to that person we thought of, according to the Word of God.

In Danny Silk's book, *Culture of Honor,* he quotes another secret which states so succinctly, what I had learned:

"We don't honor others because they are honorable; we honor them because we are honorable."

Let this truth change the way we respond to every situation we find ourselves in with others. God began to speak to me about a passage I read in the Word. While on a plane, traveling to a wedding, He confirmed this passage in a book I was reading. At the wedding, the priest read this same passage. By then, I *knew* the Lord was speaking to me and asked Him to explain what He was trying to say. He answered by asking me what honor looks like expressed to others. Then, He spoke this secret:

"Honor is not only an attitude but an action; for honor looks like something."

That passage was in Luke 6, where Jesus is teaching what is called 'The Beatitudes.' I will share those which were highlighted to me, those that exemplify honor and love expressed in actions. We will start in Luke 6:22–23 in the *Message Bible* for all verses except as noted. *The Message Bible* clarifies what Jesus was trying to convey in a language we can relate to and understand.

> *"Count yourself blessed every time someone cuts you down, excludes you, or throws you out, every time someone smears or blackens your name to discredit me. You should be glad when that happens – skip like a lamb, if you like! – for even though they don't like it, I do and all heaven applauds. And know that you are in good company; my preachers and witnesses have always been treated like this."*

We are *always* going to have those who oppose us, so the difference is not with them; the difference is with us. Paying back evil for evil or paying back evil with good? Do we count ourselves blessed when we encounter people who hate us and treat us badly? Or, do we retaliate either in word or thought? Do we judge them? I Peter 3:9 tells us we are to pay back evil with a blessing so we may inherit a blessing. This is a blessing we totally miss out on by not obeying this verse. Notice in Luke 6:23 the phrase, 'and all heaven applauds.' How many are missing out on this reward of heaven?

> *"To you who are ready for the truth, I say this: Love your enemies. Let them bring out the best in you, not the worst. Do good to those who hate you. When someone gives you a hard time, respond with blessings for that person. If someone slaps you in the face, stand there and take it. If someone grabs your shirt, giftwrap your best coat and make a present of it. If someone takes unfair advantage of you, use the occasion to practice the servant life."*
> Luke 7:27-30 (MSG)

I want to share an experience my sister had and how she put this principle into practice. She worked for a woman who owned a jewelry store, where she also used her boss' outside area for her own business, which was teaching women to paint on silk scarves. She trusted her boss and shared her heart and vision with her, concerning her desire to open an art studio.

When the owner moved locations, my sister thought it was an opportune time to venture out on her own, but also to expand her painting on scarves to include canvas and glass. Her former boss decided to open an art studio in her jewelry store, painting on scarves and canvas. This was the dream my sister shared with her the year before.

Not only did she take my sister's idea, but also accused her of stealing the idea from her. She also attempted to discredit her by telling this to other employees and customers. Even though my sister felt so betrayed, she would not speak against her former boss but instead prayed blessings over her boss' new business.

It was an extremely difficult time for my sister and walking in love and honor toward her former boss was difficult to do. A year later, her boss closed the doors of her new location while my sister's business is still going.

Here's another testimony about how to respond to those authorities who are persecuting you.

I have a friend who led a church where a mighty move of God came. The head of the denomination was also this man's former pastor. This man brought my friend before the board to give him an ultimatum to stop having certain people come to speak at his church. My friend didn't stop having those speakers come, but was led by the Lord to begin to sow financially into this man's ministry to bless him; in order to 'bless those who persecute us.' That was some years ago, and he is still in that denomination and was not removed as he thought he might have been.

We are seeing that honor actually looks like something; it is not just an attitude, but an action.

You see, heaven stood up and applauded my friend's response and moved on his behalf! He was just obeying these words from 'The Beatitudes,' spoken by Jesus. Jesus' Words are so pivotal to walking in the Kingdom of God and having the authority of heaven move on our behalf when difficult circumstances come against us.

> *"Here is a simple rule of thumb for behavior: Ask yourself what you want people to do for you; then grab the initiative and do it for them! If you only love the lovable, do you expect a pat on the back? Run–of–the–mill sinners do that. If you only help those who help you, do you expect a medal? Garden–variety sinners do that. If you lend to those from whom you hope to receive back, what credit is that to you? If you only give for what you hope to get out of it, do you think that's charity? The stingiest pawnbroker does that."*
> Luke 6:31–34 (MSG)

So, how are we to apply this verse? What is it we are waiting for and desiring? Go out and do the same thing for someone else. If we help someone and they don't return the favor or lend to someone who doesn't pay us back, how are we going to respond? Jesus said, *"If you lend to those from which you hope to receive back, what credit is it to you?"* No credit in God's eyes! We are being told to love, help, and lend to those who are difficult and unloving.

Recently the Lord reminded me that I had invested a large sum of money somewhere and was expecting to be paid back. He told me I was to cancel the debt and give them this money with no expectations of ever being paid back. At this point in my life, I know it is crucial to obey the Lord and have a good attitude about it.

We just don't know or understand what doors will open to us when we obey these principles, but God does – and He rewards obedience!

> *"I tell you, love your enemies. Help, lend, and give without*
> *expecting a return as you will be sons of the Most High.*
> *You'll never – I promise – regret it. Live out this*
> *God-created identity the way our Father lives toward*
> *us, generously and graciously, even when we're at our*
> *worst. For He is kind to the unthankful, ungrateful,*
> *and evil. Therefore, be merciful, just as*
> *your Father is merciful."*
> Luke 6:35–36 (MSG)

Choose to move from being annoyed by others, to becoming like God who is kind and merciful to the ungrateful and unthankful.

This part of the verse jumped out at me: *"For He is kind to the unthankful, ungrateful, and evil. Therefore, be merciful, just as your Father is merciful."* In thinking about how much I had given to someone who seemed to be ungrateful of what was being sown into their life and just expected it, I chose to move from being annoyed by them to becoming like God who is kind and merciful, even to the ungrateful and unthankful. Honor truly does look like something!

The verse also says, we are to love our enemies and help them! Isn't that what my friend did with his former pastor?

"For judgment is without mercy to one who has shown no mercy. Mercy triumphs over judgment."
James 2:13

**Extend mercy to others if we want mercy;
for mercy triumphs over judgment.**

Mercy is the only way to go and overcomes judgment and criticism. These scriptures are powerful and will change our life, family, church, and city if we begin to walk in Jesus' words and obey them.

These verses in Luke 6 unlock the power of the government of the Kingdom of God that the Church sometimes is missing. Many people feel it's about the gifts and power, but Jesus modeled and spoke of what the Kingdom looks like, here in these verses and many other scriptures like them. Power and gifts don't replace obedience to the difficult scriptures in the Word; instead, they greatly enhance them. Obedience adds the glory of God to our lives and opens the door to spiritual promotion like nothing else does.

"Don't pick on people, jump on their failures, criticize their faults – unless, of course, you want the same treatment. Don't condemn those who are down; that hardness will be a boomerang. Be easy on people; you'll find life a lot easier. Forgive and you will be forgiven. Give away your life; you'll find life given back, but not merely given back – given back with a bonus and blessing. Giving not getting, is the way. For with the same measure that you use, will be measured back to you."
Luke 6:37–38 (MSG)

Instead of criticizing and judging others, we need to begin to see the *'gold'* in people's lives and call that out of them. Start to see others through God's heart! When people are outwardly being difficult, see the good in them, and tell them the good you see. Speak into their destiny and calling! When they have unconditional love extended toward them, they are put into position to be transformed.

Remember, in Judges 6:12, Gideon was hiding and afraid; and in the midst of his fear, God called him a *mighty man of valor* – and he became that very thing! God saw and called the gold out of Gideon's life...

We can do this for others and see their lives transformed!

**If we walk in judgment and criticism, we
will reap the same in our life.**

When we walk in judgment, criticism, and always pointing out other's faults, we reap the same back into our own lives. In

Luke 6:38, it says with the same measure we use with others, it will be measured back to us. I'm entering into a new season of joy and finding new ways to bless and respond to people. I choose to no longer focus on weaknesses, but in speaking into people's strengths. I'm finding this new way of dealing with people creates a place of love and security, bringing freedom and safety to change. At the same time, I am continuing to ask the Lord to reveal to me any areas in my own life that don't line up with His Word, so He can transform me.

> *"It's easy to see a smudge on your neighbor's face and be oblivious to the ugly sneer on your own. Do you have the nerve to say, 'Let me wash your face for you,' when your own face is distorted by contempt? It's this I–know–better–than–you mentality again, playing a holier–than–thou part instead of just living your own part. Wipe that ugly sneer off your own face, and you might be fit to offer a washcloth to your neighbor."*
> Luke 6:41–42

How quick we are to point out others' faults and weaknesses but totally miss seeing our own. All of us have blind spots in our character that we can't see in ourselves. Instead, we need to allow the Holy Spirit to wash our lives clean in purity, so we know how to deal with others when they fail. How wonderful the Church would look by applying these truths, as the world would be drawn to such a church. For love never fails!

> *"Brethren, even if anyone is caught in a tresspass, you who are spiritual, restore such a one in the spirit of gentleness; each one looking to yourself, so that you too will not be tempted."*
> Galatians 6:1 (NASB)

If we are frustrated with someone, we will have no authority to speak into their life to see them transformed.

Restoring someone in the spirit of gentleness involves realizing, but for the grace of God goes I. God showed me some years ago that if I was frustrated with someone, I would have no authority to speak into their life to see them transformed. I needed to allow the Lord to remove my frustration first, fill me with His love for them, and then I could go and gently speak to them.

I also learned, confronting them was *not* to relieve *my* frustration to get them to stop doing whatever I was frustrated with. It was to be because I loved them and did not want to see them continue hurting themselves or others.

This is the same attitude the Lord has with us when He brings correction into our life; so we need to extend this same attitude toward others.

"For a gentle answer turns away wrath, and a harsh word stirs up anger."
Proverbs 15:1

Ephesians 4:15 says to speak the truth in love. If we try to bring correction while frustrated, people feel judged and become extremely defensive. We can't confront people to change for *our* sake, as this is self–centered. But, when we go to them because we love them and *truly* want to see them transformed *for their sake*, a gentle answer will turn away their wrath. Honor *always* looks like something!

> *"You don't get wormy apples off a healthy tree, nor good*
> *apples off a diseased tree. The health of the apple tells the*
> *health of the tree. You must begin with your own life–giving*
> *lives. It's who you are, not what you say and do, that counts.*
> *Your true being brims over into true words and deeds. For*
> *out of the abundance of the heart, the mouth speaks."*
> Luke 6:43–45 (MSG)

The fruit of our life speaks for itself, and who we are speaks to others louder than our words do. Know this: Whatever is in our heart becomes what we speak. Either we speak in gentleness and build people up, or we speak in harshness and tear them down. One is the Kingdom of God and the other is the kingdom of darkness. Sow into the Kingdom of God as we deal with other people. We are either a good tree when we speak to build them up or a bad tree when we speak to tear someone down. People will be able to tell what kind of tree we actually are, by listening to what comes out of our mouths from our heart. *For out of the abundance of our heart, our mouth speaks!*

> *"Why do you call me Lord, Lord and not do the things I say?"*
> Luke 6:46 (NKJV)

What things that he *says* is He referring to here? *The words we read in The Beatitudes!* He is saying if He is *really* Lord in our life, then we will live out these scriptures and put them into practice.

> *"If you work the words into your life, you are like a smart*
> *carpenter who dug deep and laid the foundation of his house*
> *on bedrock. When the river burst its banks and crashed*
> *against the house, nothing could shake it; it was built to last.*

But if you just use my words and don't work them into your
life, you are like a dumb carpenter who built a house but
skipped the foundation. When the swollen river came crashing
in, it collapsed like a house of cards. It was a total loss."
Luke 6:48–49 (MSG)

Too many Christians are like those who build their homes on the sand and have skipped laying the foundation, which means they either don't know, or they read, memorize, and quote the scriptures but don't live them out in their lives. Their lives are falling apart and everything seems to be going wrong. They blame it on the devil – or others – and fail to realize why all this is happening to them. They don't understand it's because they are not *living* and putting into practice what the Bible tells us we should do; not putting into *practice* the truth of the Word.

If we do what the Bible instructs us to do, our house –
our life, *will* survive the storms of life.

The New King James Version says, *"The flood arose and beat vehemently against it."* The flood can signify conflicts, so when conflicts come against us, we will either stand if we walk in these principles or immediately fall if we don't. It also says, the ruin of that house is great. If we have conflict after conflict in our home, family, work, church, or neighborhood and walk in unforgiveness, resentment, bitterness, or respond differently than what Jesus said to us in 'The Beatitudes,' our house will not stand. We will continue having no peace, where conflicts continually come against our life, and we will be miserable.

Walking in these principles will cause us to bring honor and

118

love to those who are walking opposed to us, and our life will turn around. Conflicts will still come, but we will *continually* rise above them. Remember, heaven backs those who walk in honor, as honor is an action and looks like something!

This scripture in Luke also tells us, if we obey His words, the rains or floods will come against our house, but it will stand. I know I really want my house to continue standing after the rains – the tests of life – come. Nothing will be able to shake us because our life will be unshakable, built upon the rock of *living* His Word and will outlast any storm of life we find ourselves in.

Lord, I declare the Body of Christ will receive a revelation on the importance of walking in a culture of honor with *everyone* they meet. I declare in the days to come, heaven will overtake and back *everyone* who chooses to walk in honor toward those who are worthy and – even more importantly – unworthy. I declare we will begin to obey *every* scripture in the Word of God, not just the ones we like, and that our houses will stand and last into eternity. In Jesus' name, Amen.

SECRET KINGDOM PRINCIPLES

The kind of loyalty and faithfulness that David had for Saul needs to be established in our life.

The culture of the Kingdom is built upon honor; and is essential for us, to unlock government and power in the Kingdom of God.

Honor releases heaven for supernatural miracles on our behalf.

Honor unlocks the gifts in others for impartation into *our* life.

"We don't honor others because they are honorable; we honor them because we are honorable."

"Honor is not only an attitude but an action; for honor looks like something."

Choose to move from being annoyed by others, to becoming like God who is kind and merciful to the ungrateful and unthankful.

Extend mercy to others if we want mercy; for mercy triumphs over judgment.

If we walk in judgment and criticism, we will reap the same in our life.

If we are frustrated with someone, we will have no authority to speak into their life to see them transformed.

If we do what the Bible instructs us to do, our house – our life, *will* survive the storms of life.

Chapter 7

WHO'S IN CHARGE?

"All of you must obey those who rule over you. There are no
authorities except the ones God has chosen. Those who
now rule have been chosen by God. So, whoever
opposes the authorities opposes leaders whom God
has appointed. Those who do that will be judged."
Romans 13:1–2 (NIRV)

There is a colloquialism that says, "Insanity is when you keep doing the same thing, but expect different results." This saying couldn't be more accurate when it comes to bringing us back into true Kingdom alignment. As the Body of Christ, we need to start living our lives according to what is written in the Word of God! By aligning our lives to *living* the Word, we will begin to reap transformation in our lives and circumstances.

Marios Ellinas wrote a very powerful statement in his book, *Warrior Material*:

"There is a direct correlation between submission to authority and the level of authority we obtain. The more we yield (submit) to authority, the more authority we will be granted."

If we don't embrace this truth and act upon it, we will live a life of mediocrity – or worse, miss walking in the perfect will of God for our life altogether. Another secret is:

If we say we honor authority, but don't walk in submission and obedience, we actually *dishonor* that authority.

We honor, even though we may not agree with the person in authority; or think they are in error. Just remember David and Joseph!

"Let <u>EVERY</u> soul be subject to the governing authorities. For there is <u>NO</u> authority except from God, and the authorities that exist are appointed by God. Therefore, whoever <u>RESISTS</u> the authority <u>RESISTS</u> <u>the</u> <u>ordinance</u> <u>of</u> <u>God</u>."
Romans 13:1–2 (NKJV)

To resist means to *rebel*, and in I Samuel 15:23, it tells us rebellion is as the sin of witchcraft. To resist also means to become critical because we feel it's not what we believe we are hearing God say, or we're not in agreement with the leader and become judgmental. To resist means to gossip to others about this leader because we think they are wrong – even if under the false pretense of, "I'm sharing this so you can pray for them."

To be in submission to those in authority is not merely a suggestion but a *command* from God – and that means NO ONE is exempt! It's not only in reference to governmental authority but ANY delegated authority placed over us. This means civil authority, as well as in the Church like elders and ministry leaders. It also includes a boss, parent, or *any* leader that is set over us.

God has set up spheres of authority, or places of governing, within boundaries given by the Lord to those *He has chosen* for these authority positions. We need to learn to stay within the sphere of authority we have been given and not step into another person's sphere.

For instance, if a prophet gives the Word of the Lord to someone and then attempts to make sure it is implemented or gets *upset* when others do not receive it, they are no longer walking in their own sphere of authority. They have stepped out of bounds into the sphere of the authority which belongs only to the Holy Spirit. Actually, they begin to operate in manipulation. The sphere of authority of someone who gives a prophetic word is simply to say what God is saying. They are merely the delivery person, not the author. Let's not step into rebellion or pride, and remember it is God alone who is responsible for the outcome of the word given. We need to continually guard our hearts against moving out of our sphere of authority, into someone else's sphere.

Another example of stepping out of our sphere is trying to push our own agenda and what we want to see happen when we don't agree with a leader. When we do that, we are crossing the boundary into someone else's sphere. Learning to stay within the sphere of authority *we* have been given is so *important* in Heaven's eyes.

Come under the authority of those whom God has set into that place over our lives.

"Bondservants, be obedient to those who are your masters according to the flesh, with fear and trembling, in sincerity of heart, as to Christ; not with eye–service, and men–pleasers, but as bondservants of Christ, doing the will of God from the heart, with goodwill doing service, as to the Lord, and not to men...."
Ephesians 6:5–7 (NKJV)

Ephesians 6 is mostly well–known because it is here where the apostle Paul describes the armor of God we have been given and the power it possesses when we use it. However, before he mentions one word about the armor of God, he first addresses the area of submission to authority, beginning in Ephesians 5:21 and continuing in chapter 6.

As we read this passage, we see there is a God–ordained progression of submission to authority which first begins with us submitting ourselves one to another. The progression continues, addressing wives, children, and slaves. It also addresses fathers and masters, concerning their treatment of those under their care. We have totally missed that this progression of submission is extremely important for us to obtain the armor, weapons, and training to wage effective spiritual warfare. After nine verses of instructions, Paul says in verse 10 (KJV):

"Finally, my brethren, be strong in the Lord and in the power of His might."

We need to understand that this submission is a *prerequisite* for effectively waging warfare against principalities and powers. The bottom line is: We need to be in proper submission to authority at EVERY level of God's governmental structure.

Remember the story of that Roman centurion soldier in Matthew 8? As one whose position gave him great authority over others, he recognized both the power and authority that comes from *first* submitting to authority. Through honoring and submitting to the authority over us, we *position* ourselves both to receive and exercise great authority in the Kingdom of God.

During those difficult years of being under harsh authority, had I not learned to walk in submission with an honoring attitude, God would have never been able to bring me to a new level of *greater* authority. God is testing us, trying us, and purifying us in this season. Matthew 9:17 says, He can't pour new wine into old wineskins for the next season we find ourselves in.

In reading this, maybe we are feeling discouraged about not seeing our current situation change in our favor. Or, maybe we are not walking in the destiny we know we were created for. If so, there may be areas where we have not submitted to those leaders over us, have not had a good attitude about decisions they've made, or how they've been walking. Maybe the leader has not received our words, ideas, opinions, or suggestions like we thought they should have. Prayerfully ask the Lord to reveal to us areas where we need to make a genuine commitment to fix them.

"God opposes the proud but shows favor to the humble."
James 4:6b

Is it any wonder, we are not being recognized for the giftings in our life or the ministries we have in our heart when we have grumbled against these leaders and may have even voiced our complaints to others? This is actually rebellion that originates from pride when we don't submit. The reality is, that it is actually God who is resisting us. 1 Peter 5:5 says, *"for God resists the proud, but gives grace to the humble."* This means, if we resist *any* authority placed over us, we enter into pride and then God resists *us*, because He resists the proud. He will do so until we humble *ourselves.* He will withhold the keys to the car (the fullness of destiny) *until* we come into maturity and understand how important this subject is to Him.

We may be resisted by God through a leader if we are not submitted to them.

How many of us are being resisted by God, through a leader, simply because we have not recognized these truths and are not submitted in our heart to that leader.

In the Kingdom, attitudes of the heart trump actions or words.

Maybe you have been submitted with your actions but not your heart. I am reminded of the story about a boy whose parent told him to sit down. Grudgingly, the child sat down, but only because he was made to do so by the parent. The child says to them, "I may be sitting on the outside, but I am still standing on the inside." Have we been like this with our boss, parents, or church leaders? We can be sure of one thing: God sees the attitude of our heart!

Let's take a look at the story of Korah and Moses found in Numbers 16. God placed Moses in the position of authority as the predominant leader over the Children of Israel. But, Korah, as well as 250 others, resisted Moses and basically said, "Who do you think you are? We hear from God too!" The Bible called him insolent which means: '*showing a rude and arrogant lack of respect.*' God was *upset* by his attitude and caused the ground to open, swallowing up Korah, all those associated with him, and their families. We are thankful He doesn't do that to us after Christ came, as we are now given opportunities to repent and change because of Jesus' shed blood for our sins. How many times have we been guilty of having this same attitude, "I hear from God too," when a leader does not receive our advice or do what we think should be done? We saw how God feels about this attitude! Instead of becoming upset and having a bad attitude, wouldn't it be better to submit, and pray to the Lord who has the power to change the circumstance? *If,* what we want lines up with His will! We need to *trust* God to deal with our wrong leader as we submit and pray.

More importantly, because we are walking in a submissive spirit, God will elevate us in due season to a higher level of authority. Conversely, if we don't walk in the proper honor and submission, we will be stuck where we are. We may be miserable because we don't see God's power working in us the way we would like; possibly never seeing our dreams being fulfilled. Sadly, we may *never* recognize the correlation between our lack of honoring our leader and why we are not moving forward.

Jesus was submitted to ALL authority, which gave him *great* authority!

Jesus was very effective during His lifetime on earth because He submitted Himself to *all* authority placed over Him – governmental, parental, and ultimately God's authority. Therefore, He lived and operated as one with *great* authority.

"The people were astonished at His doctrine, for He taught them as one having authority, and not as the scribes."
Matthew 7:28-29 (NKJV)

Christ's submission and obedience made a way for His disciples to access *higher* levels of authority when they were sent out to minister. As long as they were yielded and submitted to the Lord's authority, they continually grew in favor, power, gifting, understanding, and greater authority – and so it shall be with us!

Whether it's the authority figure in our home, job, a civic leader, or someone in a spiritual position over us – it really doesn't matter; God's principles remain the same. It's *our* responsibility to properly discern whether we are truly submitted, not only in word but in our hearts. It may be God's principle, but the enemy continually tries to hide this from us and lies to us. He keeps the truth veiled from us, as he wants us to rebel against authority. Satan knows if we do, we will *never* walk in the fullness and power of true Kingdom authority, the kind that will destroy his kingdom, until we have learned and obeyed these principles of submission to authority. It's that crucial!

"All of you must obey those who rule over you. There are no authorities except the ones God has chosen. Those who now rule have been chosen by God. So, whoever opposes the authorities, opposes leaders whom God has appointed. Those who do that will be judged."
Romans 13:1–2

Wow! In Romans, it tells us, "There are *no* authorities, except the ones God has chosen." Also, whoever opposes those authorities God has chosen will pay consequences. This couldn't be more straightforward! Think of our political arena surrounding the last few presidents. This verse says that if we oppose them, then we are opposing God. Yikes!

We need to remember the apostles walked in a world of *great* immorality, idolatry, hate, violence, murder and corruption, but because they understood and lived their lives by this teaching, they were able to transform the earth everywhere they went. They shifted atmospheres, and brought multitudes into the Kingdom. I would say these are the *precise* conditions we see today, as *nothing* has changed from biblical days!

"Submit yourselves for the Lord's sake to every human institution, whether to a king as the one in authority....For such is the will of God that by doing right you may silence the ignorance of foolish men. Act as free men, and do not use your freedom as a covering for evil, but use it as bond slaves of God. Honor all people, love the brotherhood, fear God, honor the king."
I Peter 2:13-17 (NASB)

We see in this scripture, this covers ALL authority in worldly government. Nero was the ruler and emperor, when the apostles walked the earth, and was as *corrupt* as they come. Yet,

Peter still said to submit to *every* human institution, whether to the king as the one in authority, but also told us to *honor the king.* This verse also says that this is the will of God! How are we talking about and acting toward *our* governmental leaders? Are we submitted to honoring them just like Peter instructed Believers to do? That's pretty easy to do if *our* candidate is in office, but this command is not conditional, as we still need to honor the Nero's as well.

"Servants, be submissive to your masters with all respect, not ONLY to those who are good and gentle, but also to those who are unreasonable."
I Peter 2:18 (KJB)

The New International Version of the Bible, tells us, *"but also to those who are harsh."* The Bible has *so much* to say about our attitudes and actions toward our leaders. We should evaluate how we are walking in this issue of authority, as there are *so* many verses regarding this subject. God makes it *extremely* clear on what our submission to authority should look like and the repercussions we can expect if we don't. We are to be in submission with ALL respect, not only to those who are good and gentle, but also to those who are unreasonable and harsh. In God's eyes, there is NO difference in how we are to respond – only according to man's eyes.

"Obey your leaders and submit to them, for they keep watch over your souls as those who will give an account. Let them do this with joy and not with grief, for this would be unprofitable for you."
Hebrews 13:17 (KJV)

This one will cover those authorities over us in the church. If we feel they are not worthy, this verse gives us comfort in knowing that *they will give an account* and will be held accountable for our soul. It also tells us *not to give them grief,* as *it would be unprofitable for US.* We don't want to live an unprofitable life, with all that opens the door to. Let's not continue to be deceived by the enemy who wants to keep us powerless by not submitting to authority, which also circum-vents the destiny God has planned for us.

We don't need to be in agreement with those leaders set over us, as we just need to honor them in the same way David did with Saul. We don't have to be door mats either as David still ran for his life, not allowing Saul to murder him. Ephesians 4:15 says, we can also speak the truth in *love* while we are submitted to them. The bottom line is, we just need to have a *good attitude* toward our leaders and *trust* God in all things.

While obeying these verses, God may intervene on our behalf, just like He did for Paul and Silas in Acts 16, when they were chained in that prison. While they were praising and singing, God rescued them because they had GREAT attitudes, and were even concerned about the poor jailor when they were set free! Remember, heaven will move on behalf of those who honor and submit to their leaders, as unto the Lord.

What the Lord has been showing me recently is those who have ears to hear what the Spirit is saying, will be walking in the *greatest* authority in the Kingdom of God. Those who don't, will be relegated to a lower position where mediocrity is the *norm*. While those who submit to authority, with a pure heart and good attitude, will be doing great exploits for the Kingdom and walking in favor with God and man. Those who refuse to do so will live in frustration, unable to figure out why they aren't walking in more power and authority.

Lord, I declare we will submit to *every* authority over us in obedience to Your Word, and will receive the reward of the blessings You give to those who do. I declare attitudes are changing and paradigm shifts are coming, so we will truly understand that by submitting, heaven opens and grants us greater authority in our lives and ministry. In Jesus' name, Amen.

SECRET KINGDOM PRINCIPLES

If we say we honor authority, yet don't walk in submission and obedience, we actually dishonor that authority.

Come under the authority of those whom God has set into that place over our lives.

We may be resisted by God through a leader if we are not submitted to them.

In the Kingdom, attitudes of the heart trump actions or words.

Jesus was submitted to ALL authority, which gave him *great* authority!

Chapter 8
PROTOCOLS

"Whoever can be trusted with very little can also be trusted with much, and whoever is dishonest with very little will also be dishonest with much."
Luke 16:10

When my husband and I were called to move and came to the church we now attend, I went to the senior leader and told him, "I submit myself under your authority for as long as I'm in this house."

Even though I walk in an apostolic authority, that authority is only given to me within the sphere the Lord gives me to operate in that capacity. The Lord has given the sphere of authority in this church to my senior leader. Ouch, if we are not mindful of this!

To walk as a *true* leader, we need to learn to not promote

ourselves or our ministries, but instead, submit to the divine order of the church or ministry we're in, serve the leader's vision, and wait for the Lord to promote us in His own time. I came into this church, took a back seat, and waited for the Lord to tell me what my next assignment would be.

I sat waiting for two *necessary* years – God knew more transformation was needed for the *next* assignment I found myself in. The Lord needed to prepare me for the next season of ministry and I found myself in another cave experience!

There is a season of being *concealed*, to bring us into more maturity, before being *revealed* again in the next assignment the Lord has for us. This is the way of the Kingdom to prepare us for our next season of destiny being released!

I am asking all of us to evaluate our lives and allow the Holy Spirit to reveal to us those areas where we have not been submitted to the authority figures God has placed over us. Then, if we need to go and confess this to our present leader – or even a past leader – we should be willing to do whatever the Lord leads us to do in order to make things right. Remember, I went back to several past leaders to ask their forgiveness for judging them.

It's important to take responsibility to do the right thing, by going back to clean up the messes we have made with people.

Obedience to this command is pretty *radical*, but it will revolutionize our life if we are willing. The Kingdom will flow into our life in ways we have not understood or experienced before. Everything the Lord has planted in our heart to do will have the authority of God behind it. Such awesome and wondrous blessings are attached to this powerful Kingdom secret. Let us grab hold of this truth and allow it to transform our life.

We need to understand the protocol of the Kingdom in which greater things come from serving the lesser things, as God promotes faithful people.

Luke 16:10 tells us, if God can trust us with a little, He will give us more and greater things, because God promotes faithful people. The problem is we become too focused on our *own* calling, gifting, and anointing. There will always be those, who are not noticed soon enough to be given a position or platform and end up leaving. We all probably know some people who go from Church to Church until they find one that will give them a platform. Sadly, this comes at the cost of true Kingdom greatness and authority.

When we realize and understand our mandate, move in rank, and wait for the Lord's promotion, heaven's authority will be behind *everything* we say and do.

Did you know your rank and submission to authority is clearly seen by the powers of darkness? Rank and authority must come into our lives to have great authority over those realms of darkness. Rank comes from submitting to authority, knowing what place we have been given in the Body of Christ, and *staying* within that sphere of authority. The enemy always submits to the highest power in the room. If it's heaven's power operating in us by submission to authority, then we become the highest power. If not, the powers of darkness become the highest power and they won't submit to us as one having authority. We need to understand how important authority is in the supernatural realm, as *both* heavenly and demonic realms operate in and under authority.

I encourage us all to begin to understand the absolute importance of what I am sharing!

BECOMING A WARRIOR

I shared with you in the first chapter, the three–year revival we experienced. Each week, in our living room, we were seeing the power of God manifesting through signs and wonders. During this season, the Holy Spirit led me into a deliverance ministry. However, the only model I saw was people screaming at demons for hours when they tried to deliver people. The problem was, I didn't see that model in the Word of God. So, I began to cry out to God for direction.

He began to show me that if I dealt with the root issue of why the demon had a place to operate, they would have no choice but to comply and leave. I entered into a successful deliverance ministry after this revelation. Here is one example of what the Lord showed me in a frantic call I received one night.

I met with this young couple after the wife had picked up a gun and almost shot her husband. She told me she regularly saw herself hovering over her body, watching herself wash the dishes. She constantly heard voices talking to her about so many things, but also in telling her to get a gun and kill her husband. When I asked the Lord to show us the root issue of her demonic stronghold, it was revealed that when she was young, her father would hold séances in their home. She was curious and would sit on the stairs and watch; this is where the demons began to oppress her life. I led her in a prayer of repentance for participating with the occult and we closed the door that had been opened at that time. After praying, I spoke to those demons and they came out quickly. They knew, because we removed their legal access through repentance, they could not stay. Twenty years later, I saw her sister who told me she never had any further demonic problems after that night. She was still walking free!

The problem that emerged later in my life, and one so many Christians struggle with, is that everything I saw happening which was negative, I blamed on the devil. I was binding and loosing *everything* during that season. Sadly, the attacks continued and I assumed this was normal Christian life. Many others told me they were constantly being attacked by the enemy, especially before attending spiritual meetings. Whenever anything went wrong, we would see it as a demonic attack and this mentality *always* led to a defeated attitude.

Something changed all this type of thinking! When I was called to start that national women's ministry, I was led to pray at the Capitol building. There, I saw a huge demon straddling the dome, how it was dressed, and knew its name. I also knew it was the ruling authority over our state and was operating in the seat of government at the Capitol. I heard the Lord say to me, "This one will not be dealt with by binding and loosing." I didn't understand what He meant and didn't do anything about this vision. It would take a few years to gain understanding.

Some years later, an international speaker came to a house meeting I attended. I told him about this ruling demon and asked if he had picked up on what the prevailing demonic strongholds were, when he came into our area. I was totally taken by surprise when he told me I was asking the wrong question. He said, "Instead of asking what the demonic strong-hold is over the region, you should be asking what God and the angels are doing in the region and begin to partner with them." Wow! That changed my entire perspective.

That which we *focus* on, we give power to!

I also heard a teaching that changed how I saw all of this. The Lord impressed me with this thought: "That which you focus on, you give power to." This statement revealed another se-cret, where I came to realize I was focusing *way* too much on what I thought the devil was doing, and by doing so, I was actually giving him *more* power. This was just what he wanted! I also came to realize, not every negative thing that happens is an attack of the devil. There are trials in life we all have! In-stead of focusing on what the demonic realm was doing, I *began* to focus on what God was doing in the midst of every circumstance I found myself in.

I also came to realize, that by focusing my attention on the darkness and what the enemy was doing, I had been placing the devil as an equal to God. Satan is equal with the angels and is no match for our God who created him. Life did a 180 – degree turn for me! No more was I giving power to the darkness, but started on a journey to seeing what God was doing and began focusing my heart on that.

This transformed all the defeat in my life into a road of victory!

"Truly I tell you, whatever you bind on earth will be bound in heaven, and whatever you loose on earth will be loosed in heaven."
Matthew 18:18

The Spirit revealed to me the '*binding*' and '*loosing*' in this verse wasn't meant to be literal but *figurative*. I had been taught to say, "I bind you," when dealing with the realms of darkness. He revealed, it really meant that whatever we don't allow is 'binding,' and whatever we do allow is 'loosing.' From that point on, I changed how I ministered. If we receive revelation from the Lord, we are *accountable* to change. I saw in the Word that Jesus *never* used the words, bind or loose, when addressing demons. He just commanded them to leave!

I would speak in a manner to not allow sickness, demons, or any form of darkness to prevail. I also began to speak God's provision for these things to be manifested in the natural, like healing, freedom, or finances. This revelation began the ministry of *declaring,* in order to bring heaven to earth. Declarations are not us, asking God to do something; they are declaring them already done! Romans 4:17 tells us, God calls the things that were not, as though they were.

In a Leader's meeting, a woman told me she saw a huge demon who was assigned to me. She also said it was standing near me and emphasized I needed to address it. I pressed into the Lord to know how to handle what the woman instructed me to do. He said, "Don't address it; worship Me, and see what happens." I began to declare the power of God and His goodness, and it slowly began to shrink until it became the size of a mouse. All that was needed was to step on it and it was gone. God was teaching me that by focusing on *Him,* rather than the demon, it lost its power and authority in my life.

This was another turning point and training for what was to come!

Kingdom secrets lead us deeper into understanding how to operate successfully to access true Kingdom authority.

For many years, I didn't do anything about the demon I saw over the capitol until the Lord called me to start the regional ministry, with my apostolic and prophetic team. I wouldn't have been able to be called into this type of ministry, unless I had first learned to submit to *all* authority – especially during that season of harsh leaders. All these lessons were *extremely* necessary to be able to walk in the kind of authority that would be required for this new assignment. I needed *all* of this training before being able to deal with ruling demons over the region.

WHO TOLD YOU?

In Genesis 3, Adam and Eve had eaten from the one and only

forbidden tree in the middle of the Garden of Eden, after being specifically told by God not to. We know the story that after they ate and realized what they had done, they hid from the Lord. When God went looking for them, He called out to Adam, asking, "Where are you?" Adam replied he was hiding, and the Lord asked him why. Adam's response was, "I was afraid because I was naked."

Who told you?

Then, God answered him, "Who told you.....that you were naked?" You see, Adam and Eve had *always* been naked, but until that moment it never was a cause of shame. It was Satan who sold them a bill of goods in revealing their nakedness and putting shame on them.

Too many times we hear voices in our head and think they are our own original thoughts. These voices may say, "It can't be done," "I am not liked or accepted," "I'm not smart enough," "Things never work out," "God can't forgive me," and so many other negative, hindering thoughts that bombard our mind. We believe these voices and receive them because we think it's our *own* voice in our head. The truth is, the enemy is speaking these lies to us. We have to retrain our mind to ask ourselves this question: "Who told me _____?" Fill in the blank with what you hear in our own head.

In *recognizing* the enemy's voice in our mind, there is freedom to reject those thoughts and replace them with the truth of who God says we are.

God didn't tell Adam he was naked; Satan did – and he is still telling us the same thing today in order to keep us from knowing who we really are in Christ and what God has freely given us. We need to learn how to take every thought captive and make it obedient to Christ, as it tells us in 2 Corinthians 10:5. Satan is so *fearful* that if we really understood who we were and what power and authority we actually carry, we would *greatly* damage his kingdom. He also knows that he would lose his hold on people, cities, regions, and nations, so he lies to us!

First, we need to understand we are even in a battle – the battle of our minds – in order to have the victory. Always remember to ask ourselves, "Who told me _____?" when negative thoughts come into our mind.

I am continually seeking for more revelations about the Word of God, in order to turn away from over 45 years of beliefs where other people taught me what *they* believed the Bible said. It's a process and I'm truly looking forward to receiving more revelations which are reserved for those who are willing to pay the price to obtain these secrets.

Lord, I declare we will walk in absolute submission to everyone You have set into leadership positions over our lives. Also, those who have a teachable heart will leave their old ways of thinking and the things they have been taught by the traditions of men. I also declare, no longer will we focus on the powers of darkness and giving them more power, but will begin to give our focus to what God is doing in every circumstance we find ourselves in. Finally, we will come into a new revelation of who we are and how the Kingdom of God operates. In Jesus' name, Amen.

SECRET KINGDOM PRINCIPLES

It's important to take responsibility to do the right thing, by going back to clean up the messes we have made with people.

We need to understand the protocol of the Kingdom in which greater things come from serving the lesser things, as God promotes faithful people.

When we realize and understand our mandate, move in rank and wait for the Lord's promotion, heaven's authority will be behind everything we say and do.

That which we *focus* on, we give power to!

Kingdom secrets lead us deeper into understanding how to operate successfully to access true Kingdom authority.

Who told you?

In *recognizing* the enemy's voice in our mind, there is freedom to reject those thoughts and replace them with the truth of who God says we are.

Chapter 9

CREATIVE POWER

"For as he thinks within himself, so he is."
Proverbs 23:7 (NASB)

I like to paraphrase this scripture: What a man thinks in his heart, that's what he is. Years ago, I *always* had the feeling that something awful was going to happen. I felt this way because I looked at everything negatively and walked in such a powerful, foreboding spirit with a great spirit of dread. The definition of *foreboding* is: *'fearful apprehension; a feeling that something bad will happen.'* It was accompanied by a tight feeling in the pit of my stomach.

I didn't understand that my beliefs and words were opening the door for the enemy to wreak havoc in my life. I cried out to the Lord as I was so tired of being someone who always saw the glass *half-empty* and wanted more than anything to be someone who saw the glass as *half-full*. The Lord delivered me from that foreboding spirit and started me on a journey of renewing my mind to line up with the Word of God.

Job was a man who constantly walked in fear his children would do something that displeased the Lord. Because of his fear, he would offer up sacrifices daily on their behalf.

> *"Job would make arrangements for them (his children) to be purified. Early in the morning, he would sacrifice a burnt offering for each of them, thinking, 'Perhaps my children have sinned and cursed God in their hearts.' This was Job's regular custom."*
> Job 1:5

Satan knew about Job's fear and saw an opportunity to wreak havoc in *his* life. He went before God to talk to Him about Job and told God that Job served Him merely because He had a wall of protection around him. Satan asked God if he could test him, and God agreed – but with one limitation: Satan could not take Job's life. Satan didn't take his life, but he did take the lives of all his children. Why was this the first thing he did? Because of Job's overwhelming fear for his children! Here, we see another Kingdom secret in operation:

As we think in our heart, so we are.

> *"What I feared the most has come upon me; what I dreaded has happened to me."*
> Job 3:25

My foreboding spirit was full of dread, just like Job. We need to understand, our fear gives Satan the power to do the very thing we fear. Because I thought in my heart, all my life, *"Something awful is about to happen,"* guess what? Terrible things happened! At that time I didn't understand, my thinking and words were a magnet to fulfill the very thing I was thinking. It wasn't until I dealt with my fear that things began to change. It's so true: change your thinking, and you will change your life!

> *"Death and life are in the power of the tongue, and those who love it and indulge it will eat its fruit and bear the consequences of their words."*
> Proverbs 18:21 (AMP)

Words that bring death are spoken and released through what we first think and then speak. This scripture is not speaking necessarily of physical death here, but words that lead to fear, anger, control, jealousy, guilt, condemnation, shame, hatred, and everything else we first think in our mind and then speak. According to this verse, we will bear the *consequences* of our words. What does that actually mean?

I began to understand how our words give power to either the kingdom of darkness or the Kingdom of God. When we think or speak words of death, we release – or give – our authority to bring to us those things we think or speak. The powers of darkness delight in our words of death, as Satan is all too willing to use them against us, just as he did Job. Our words give him permission or authority to do the things we declare out of our mouths. As a result, we begin to pay the consequences for those words.

What are these words of death? They are *all* the *negative* words we think and speak over ourselves, our family, circumstances, and others.

*"The thief comes only to steal and kill and destroy. I came that
they may have life and have it abundantly."*
John 10:10

Satan is that thief! Through our words, we give him access to
come into our lives by the words of death we speak. This allows him to steal, kill, and destroy our joy, money, blessings,
relationships, faith, trust, health, life, destiny, as well as so
much more. We *always* pay the consequences of our words.

Years ago, I read the scripture where Jesus said He came for
me to have life more abundantly, yet I *never* experienced that
abundant life. I *hated* everything about my life because I walked in a spirit of fear and looked at everything from a negative
viewpoint. My thoughts were, "Others have gifts, but I can't
walk in them," "Why does everything bad always happen to
me?" "Why can't I seem to ever get ahead?" "People don't like
me," and so many other thoughts that led to death. I was thinking negative thoughts about myself and never understood that
my words had the power to bring those *exact* things into my
life.

I was so tired of living in defeat and wanted the victory I read
about in the Word of God. Then, the Lord brought me into an
understanding of how much power my words actually held. He
began to show me a new way of thinking!

*"So, God created mankind in His own image, in the image of God
He created them; male and female He created them."*
Genesis 1:27

Years ago, I used to wonder how we were created in His own
image since we don't look like God. I pressed in to find out
how we were like Him and one day I came to the revelation of

one of those ways and found another secret.

We have the same creative power in *our* words that God does.

In Genesis 1:3, He said, *"Let there be light,"* and there was light. Whatever He spoke was created, and whatever He said came to be. He began to show me if my words lined up with the truth in the Word of God, then when spoken from my mouth, they had the same power in them to create the very words spoken. This truth began to set my life free! While I can't say I walk in this perfectly, my walk is as different as day and night. We need to grab hold of this truth, as it will transform our lives, as well as the lives of others.

Further, God led me to realize *all* my words have creative power, not just the Word of God I spoke. Remember, as a man thinks (or speaks) in his heart, so he is. This scripture revolutionized my life, and I have never been the same!

The bottom line is, *whatever* we believe and speak, so we are! For a period of about five years, no illnesses – such as colds, sore throats, or flu–like symptoms – would stay in my body because I would speak to them and not allow them access. The Lord was training me to understand the power of my words and I began to speak words of life. I realized when I had thoughts like, "I feel a cold coming on," it gave the cold permission to take over my body.

149

**When we speak the words of life with faith,
dramatic things begin to happen.**

When we speak the words of life, everything in heaven and earth begins to align with the words we say, and it's so amazing how this works. Sadly, the same power is released by our words of death. Let us turn away from those death–producing words and begin speaking words of life. In order to do that, we need to begin *thinking* words of life since our mouth will *only* speak what originates in our thinking.

Now that we understand how our negative thoughts and words are agreeing with the kingdom of darkness, which negative thoughts and words do we need to come out of agreement with? We *desperately* need to renew our minds and move out of negativity as it pertains to us, our circumstances, and others. Here is a great scripture to put into practice to begin speaking words of life.

"Finally, brothers and sisters, whatever is true, whatever is noble, whatever is right, whatever is pure, whatever is lovely, whatever is admirable – if anything is excellent or praiseworthy – think about such things."
Philippians 4:8

If our thoughts are of truthful words and are noble, right, pure, lovely, admirable, excellent, or praiseworthy, then *as we think in our heart, so we are!* One day while ministering this truth to someone, the Lord showed me a large hand which was painting on a canvas. I heard Him say:

"Just as the artist does with paint, you create your world by the words you speak."

"With the tongue we bless our Lord and Father, and with it we curse men, who have been made in God's likeness. Out of the same mouth come blessing and cursing. My brothers, this should not be!"
James 3:10 (BSB)

We have the power to bless others or curse them! We need to *truly* understand the significance of releasing a blessing or curse and the consequences we pay for what comes out of our mouth. What world are *we* creating? Is it a world we want to live in? To really understand the ramifications of what we speak and the power it gives for life or death to happen all around us is extremely important!

"A good man out of the good treasure of his heart brings forth that which is good; and an evil man out of the evil treasure of his heart brings forth that which is evil: for out of the abundance of the heart his mouth speaks."
Luke 6:45 (NKJV)

We store all our beliefs, feelings, past experiences, relationships, and everything else pertaining to our life, in our heart. From these, we either speak from the good treasure which brings life or the evil treasure that brings death. For out of the abundance of our heart, our mouth *will* speak. So, let's begin choosing life! If we are having a really difficult time doing this, there may be things that need to be healed. There are ministries out there that offer inner healing which will help you.

151

By all means, seek your healing!

"This day I call the heavens and the earth as witnesses against you that I have set before you life and death, blessings and curses. Now choose life, so that you and your children will live."
Deuteronomy 30:19

God tells us in this verse that He has set before us life and death, blessings and curses. Then He *commands* us to choose life so we and our families will live. Our families are under the words we speak over them and about them. We need to begin speaking to them words of love, encouragement, acceptance, and those that build them up.

I have seen dramatic changes in my relationship with my children. My need to control things and people in my life has been removed. I became less critical and more understanding in allowing my children to make their own adult decisions without my interference or strong opinions. Because I was learning to walk in this renewed way, I began to see them transformed and our relationships healed. I became mindful of the words I spoke and tried to put myself in their shoes, rather than react and respond with words of death. It is tough to do at times, but I can honestly say my relationship with them is so much better than it was years ago, and with less conflict. I believe as we are being transformed, it filters down to our children where there is now life, love, and safety for them to also be transformed. God has always been a generational God and is referred to as "The God of Abraham, Isaac, and Jacob." He *always* thinks and works generationally.

"As it is written, …. the God who gives life to the dead and calls into being what does not yet exist."
Romans 4:17 (BSB)

We can call things into existence that do not yet exist.

We have been made in the image of God, and He gives life to the dead. We also, according to Matthew 10:8, have been given the same power to raise the dead. This has been happening since the Old Testament, throughout the entire New Testament, and is still happening today. It then, goes without saying the second part of that verse is also for us today, which tells us we have the same creative power God does to calls things into existence that currently do not exist.

I also came to understand there is a different way to pray. I learned when God impresses me to pray what He has put upon my heart, I no longer ask Him to do it, but declare it done. I also believe what I am saying will bring that very thing into existence, as it tells us in Romans 4:17. Coincidentally, it was this very teaching that prepared me for the regional ministry that was to come later.

For example, instead of asking for our son to be set free from a bondage, declare or decree he is free from whatever has him bound. Speak those things that are not visible in his life as though they are. Speak the words the Lord gives us to say, having complete faith in knowing when we speak, the very thing we say is released in heaven and then brought to earth. We are told in Matthew 6, to pray as in The Lord's Prayer, *"on earth as it is in heaven."* When making declarations of truth, the angels are released from heaven to bring to pass that which we create by the words we speak. We will address angels and how they operate in the next chapter. This same process happens with the negative words we speak, as they are released into the realm of darkness and bring death. Job 22:28 says that if we decree a thing, it shall be established! Decree means: *'an official statement that something must happen.'* Which kingdom are we decreeing into and establishing, by our words?

> *"For by your words you will be justified, and by your*
> *words you will be condemned."*
> Matthew 12:37 (ESV)

The word *condemn* actually means: *'judgment or to pronounce a sentence.'* When we speak words of death, we condemn ourselves to a life of bad health, poverty, lack, depression, hopelessness, fear, defeat, and more. It all depends on what words come out of our mouth! We really need to be careful what we are pronouncing over ourselves, our family, our job, circumstances, and our church.

Here is another scripture the Lord gave me in regard to my words: it has literally transformed my thinking and life. The words, in parenthesis, are what God actually said to me!

> *"See, I will make you (your mouth) into a threshing sledge, new*
> *and sharp, with many teeth. You will thresh the mountains and*
> *crush them, and reduce the hills to chaff."*
> Isaiah 41:15

I sought the Lord for years before coming to fully understand the significance of this verse. I began by researching what a threshing sledge was and found it was an ancient farming tool used to harvest wheat. It was a flat platform made of wood with sharp stones and broken glass on the bottom. A man would sit on top of it while the oxen would pull it over a wheat field. The weight of the man, along with the stones and glass, would cause the stalk of wheat to be crushed, resulting in the wheat being separated. The chaff (parts not desired) would be blown away by the wind, as it weighed much less than the wheat. This was the process for the wheat being harvested.

Like this farming tool, God makes our *mouth* into a threshing sledge to thresh and crush mountains. The Lord revealed that these mountains were powers of darkness. It also says, we will reduce the hills, which are the strongholds in people's lives, to chaff; and they will be blown away in the wind. All of this is accomplished by the words of our mouth; that threshing sledge with new, many, and sharp teeth, as we create it into existence.

The words coming from our mouth have power and authority to crush the powers of darkness (mountains) and remove strongholds (hills) in our lives and the lives of others. That's *awesome* power He gives to those who understand the creative power in the words they speak! When we really grasp this truth, we will transform every place we believe and speak. I am not talking about the *'name it* and *claim it'* doctrine but about speaking the words God gives us and also from His promises, found in the Word of God. Remember this secret:

**Speak words of life, and life will happen
all around us!**

Lord, I declare we will stop speaking words of death, creating a world we don't want to live in. Instead, we will start speaking words of life to create a world that aligns us with the Word of God, wherein we will see healings, relationships restored, salvation released, resources supplied, the power of God moving, and so much more. Thank you, as we are created in Your image, and given the same creative power in our words that You have. I declare that no longer will we be speaking words of death by sowing those words into the kingdom of darkness, but we will speak the words of life and sow into the Kingdom of God. I declare that all will come to understand, the world *we* create is in the power of *our* tongue! In Jesus' name, Amen.

SECRET KINGDOM PRINCIPLES

As we think in our heart, so we are.

We have the same creative power in *our* words that God does.

When we speak the words of life with faith, dramatic things begin to happen.

"Just as the artist does with paint, you create your world by the words you speak."

We can call things into existence that do not yet exist.

Speak words of life, and life will happen all around us!

Chapter 10

MINISTRY WITH ANGELS

"Bess the LORD, you His angels, mighty in strength, who perform His word, obeying the voice of His word! Bless the Lord, all His hosts, His ministers, who do His will."
Psalm 103:20–21 (NASB)

There was a prophetic word spoken to me which I didn't understand at the time, but was about to come to pass in this new season God was bringing me into. This prophetic word said that I already knew everything I needed to know about the realms of darkness, but the Lord was going to begin to teach me how to co–labor with the angels. I knew little at that time about ministering with angels, but treasured this word and anticipated the day when this would take place.

Some years ago when called into the local regional ministry, I began to seek the Lord as to how to dismantle the ruling demon I had seen years before over the capitol. You remember, the Lord told me it wasn't going to be about binding and loosing, but this would be about hearing and doing what the Lord gave us to do for the region. He told me when this ruling demon was overturned, not only would the capital city be set free but also the entire state since this was the seat of Satan's government to rule within the state.

I want to take a moment to explain why regional transformation is needed. The reason a region doesn't see a move of God come is because the powers of darkness have been given legal access to that area from past generations' sins. It's those demonic structures that have been placed over the region, state, or nation that must be dismantled. When they are torn down, the Lord comes with a move of the Spirit into that area once belonging to darkness. A good example is, when a missionary goes to Africa to preach the Gospel for twenty years, and only sees a handful of people come to the Lord during that entire time. The reason is that particular area was given over to darkness because of the occult, crimes, sexual perversions, and murder that had been in the land for *so* many generations. The result stemming from that, is great illness, poverty, oppresssion, and crime is entrenched in that region. Also, *hardness* of heart takes place which leaves the people greatly oppressed with an inability to turn to God. When those ruling demonic structures are dismantled and their legal access is destroyed, that same missionary may now see a great move of God come; with an entire town turning to the Lord.

At that time in our capital city, a Christian senator contacted one of our Christian leaders to gather other leaders to come to the capitol to pray once a month in a legislative room, and I was invited to join them. As we prayed, the Lord began to show me things and strategies, usually through visions in the Spirit. People would be praying, and the Spirit would show me things from a different perspective. I never imagined being in a legislative room praying with state leaders, those many years prior, when I saw that huge demon straddling the capitol dome.

> *"Are not the angels ministering spirits, sent to serve those who will inherit salvation?"*
> Hebrews 1:14 (NASB)

Angels are ministering spirits sent to serve *us*.

One of the many highlights of this regional ministry is a result of a vision which came to me while we were in our office near the capitol. In this vision, I saw so many angels jammed together against a *huge* wooden fence with a very *wide* gate. There were so many of them that I couldn't see the breadth nor depth of them. I heard the Spirit say, "Open the gate and release them," so I did and the angels flew out all over the city and surrounding area. I asked the Lord how many there were and what they were sent to do. He replied, "You released a myriad (10,000), and they are the angels who gather who are being sent to remove every stumbling block out of the way."

This is an example of the kind of strategies we were given for the regional transformation! There were days when we would come into the office and find angel feathers in the room. The Holy Spirit told me while we weren't there, the angels were being sent out to accomplish the things we spoke and were shown; the things God had instructed us to do. We also had a heavenly portal in one corner of our office, where the angels ascended and descended from the heavenly realm to earth and

159

back. You could literally feel the realm of heaven when you stood beneath it.

Two weeks after releasing that myriad of angels, a nationally well–known speaker came to our area for a conference. Because we were previously acquainted, I greeted him. He was very excited as I stood there absolutely *amazed* when he told me that he had been coming into our area for over twenty years, but this time when he stepped off the plane, he was so encouraged because he had *never* seen so many angels here before. I didn't share with him about the release of those angels but treasured in my heart what he said, confirming that what we were doing was extremely significant. Sometime later, the Lord revealed to me some changes we were seeing come to our state were a direct result of our ministry and the ministry of others who were also called there. One change we saw was in the relationships of the local pastors in our capital area. In prior years, the pastors of the diverse local churches were not willing to come together to meet. However, shortly after this angelic vision, they began getting together once a month for a night of worship. For over a year, these pastors crossed denominational lines to gather together – and to this day, they still gather. Remember, the Lord told me that the angels were sent to remove stumbling blocks out of the way!

The Lord also showed me, although we were working covertly, all the churches and ministries in the area would reap the benefit of the work we were doing in the capital city. They wouldn't know how or even why things had changed, but they would reap the fruit of our secret labor. While I was in that ministry, I *never* mentioned the work we did there, nor did I tell anyone this fruit was attributed to the release of those angels.

Recently, an apostolic friend of ours came to speak at our School of Supernatural Ministry. I shared with him the testimony about the angels being released over the city. In the midst of sharing this testimony with him, he saw my entire vision as I was relating it. He proceeded to tell me that my vision answered a prayer he had been inquiring God about. He had been wondering why the pastors would get together in our state when his own neighboring state had great resistance to the idea of meeting together. I hadn't said anything to him about the fruit this vision had yielded and once again treasured in my heart what he said to confirm what I had heard years earlier. Because of his confirmation to what I had secretly held in my heart, I now feel free to share this to encourage those who are *called* to bring transformation in their own regions.

Remember, the strategies given to us will be different than what will be given to others. God knows what is needed for each city, region, or nation! It isn't a *formula*, but in being called to that city, region, or nation to bring regional transformation, we will hear what the Lord says to do.

"Bless the LORD, you his angels, mighty in strength, who <u>perform</u> <u>His</u> <u>word</u>, obeying the voice of His word! Bless the Lord, all His hosts, His ministers, who do His will."
Psalm 103:20–21 (NASB)

Angels are ministers who bring the Word of God to pass.

I had faith to believe when I spoke by the Spirit, that which I had spoken was created into existence by the words of my mouth. This caused angels to be released to accomplish what had been spoken. They performed His Word given to us!

Since our landlord gave us the ministry office rent–free, he offered us a different space, as he needed our office to rent to one of his larger clients. This new space had previously belonged to a musician who operated a recording studio, but had been evicted. The office was in such poor condition, and we had to paint before moving in. I knew the space was also in bad spiritual condition since there was a lot of drug activity that went on there. So, when we held our first meeting, I told my team we needed to spiritually clean the space. Before we could even begin, the Lord interrupted me and said, "You don't need to clean the space because while you were physically preparing the office, my angels were taking care of the spiritual cleaning." The Lord revealed that angels are sent from the throne of God to clear the way for those who are called to do what He has anointed them to do.

Several years ago, in our School of Supernatural Ministry, the Lord gave me another angelic vision. In this new vision, I was standing in heaven and the Lord handed me a large white feather. I began to do a ballet–type dance while waving this feather, and silver particles began flowing out in a stream from the end of it. As I danced, an angel followed me around with a silver bowl and filled it with the silver particles pouring out of my feather. When his bowl was filled, he left to go to earth, and another angel took his place. When this next angel's bowl was filled, he also left for earth. This pattern continued with the angels coming and going as their bowls were filled. The more I danced, the more the angels came and went to the earth. I asked the Lord what the silver was that was flowing from the end of the feather, and He told me it was the ministry of reconciliation that had been given to me.

"All of this is from God, who reconciled us to Himself through Christ and gave us the ministry of reconciliation that God was reconciling the world to Himself in Christ, not counting people's sin against them. And He has committed to us the message of reconciliation."
I Corinthians 5:18

I looked up the definition of reconciliation and found it meant: to *'restore friendly relations'* between God and man. According to the scripture above, my heavenly vision is for everyone.

We are given the power to restore *friendly relations* between God and man; and man with man.

My understanding of this vision is that I have a mandate on my life and am called to reconcile man back to God. He had *friendly relations* with Adam, but man lost it after The Fall. Thankfully, Jesus came and through His death on the cross *restored friendly relations* between God and man once again. We need to understand that God isn't wrathful, as *'God is love.'* The verse above, also said that God was not counting people's sin against them, but reconciled them to Himself in Christ.

Too many people are focused on God's wrath and misrepresent Him. They fail to understand He is reserving that wrath for those who will be thrown into the Lake of Fire at the end of the age, spoken of in Revelation 20:13–15. However, in the here and now, the Word of God says:

"If anyone hears my words but does not keep them, I do not judge

that person. For I did not come to judge the
world, but to save the world."
John 12:47 (ESV)

"God did not send His son into the world to judge the world,
but that the world might be saved through Him."
John 3:17 (NASB)

When he says something twice in the same Gospel, it means we need to pay close attention, as this is important. He is not judging us! Not only are we to *restore friendly relations* between God and man, but also to reconcile family members one to another; *to restore friendly* relations between people.

In regard to the angels in my vision, the Lord said, when He gives me something to declare (speak) or when I am ministering to others, His ministering angels are released from heaven to accomplish what I speak on earth to bring reconciliation. If we only knew and understood how the heavenly realm works on behalf of the earthly, it would make such a huge difference in how we minister and do what He has called us to do on earth. Because we don't actually *see* angels, we don't really understand their ministry to us and through us or how they work on our behalf. We can co–labor with them to accomplish the work of the Kingdom; however to do so, we need to understand the anointing we carry and the authority given to us by heaven. Otherwise, the angels who are assigned to us stand there, waiting for us to give them their next assignment. Those assignments are given when we speak the Word of God, as well as in the things the Holy Spirit tells us to declare and decree.

We had so many prophetic words, visions, declarations, instructions, and strategies given to us during that season in our regional ministry. It was actually during that season, I came to understand the angels were accomplishing *everything* we were sent there to do.

Another time, the Spirit showed me there was a certain demonic stronghold in our city. It originated from another country in Europe, went into Canada, entered the United States through a northern state closer to Canada, and then was released to our city. I received instructions to go to that state, to the very spot He revealed to me. The Lord instructed me to simply cut off communication lines from there to our capital city. As a prophetic team member and I were driving north, while still in an adjoining state, the weather become really fierce. Lightning filled the heavens, the sky turned ominously black, extremely loud thunder rolled, and a torrential rain came down. We spoke to the weather and commanded it to stop! The moment we arrived at our destination, everything came to an abrupt halt, and we were able to get out of the car and do what the Lord had called us to do, as it stayed dry the *entire* time we were there. The *moment* we stepped back into the car, the rains started again. For the *entire* drive home, there were *no* sounds of thunder or black skies, but we saw so many *lightning flashes* that we eventually stopped counting after fifty. I knew in my spirit this was supernatural, but had no understanding of what we were seeing.

The Spirit revealed to me later, those lightning flashes were the angels being dispatched, cutting all the communication lines between where we were and our capital city. We came to understand so much during that season and had success in *whatever* the *Spirit* led us to do!

Intercessors are so important to regional transformation but do not have the same *type* of assignment we had in the city.

Please understand, the work can't be done without intercessors praying; they are extremely *crucial* to the Lord's work.
There were those who were called to intercede for our assignment as well as those who had been called to intercede
specifically for the city. *All* are needed and used to prepare a
city or region for a move of God, but He also calls apostolic and
prophetic leaders, giving them mantles and spheres of authority for the city or region they are *called* to. We need to make
sure we don't try to tackle taking regions without a direct call
from God to do so. It would be very dangerous for us to take on
regional, demonic rulers without the calling, anointing, and
mantle give to us by God for that assignment.

**Demonic rulers know and recognize those who have true
authority *given* to them by God for a region,
and those who don't.**

Remember what happened to the seven sons of Sceva in the
book of Acts when they tried to cast out demons? This is what
the demon's response was.

*"But the evil spirit answered them, 'Jesus I know, and Paul I
know, but who are you?"*
Acts 19:15

In verse 16, they viciously attacked the seven men. Needless
to say, it's dangerous to take on cities or regions if we are not
called by God and He hasn't given us the authority for that
assignment. This isn't the same as casting demons out of
people, which we are *all* called to do as believers in Mark
16:17. Apostles and prophets are given a *specific* government-

tal authority needed to displace ruling spirits over a region; to prepare that area for a move of God. The example we clearly see in the New Testament is, it was the *apostles*, along with the prophets, that were sent out to take cities, regions, and nations.

"After the <u>Holy Spirit</u> <u>prevented</u> them from speaking the word in the province of Asia, they traveled through the region of Phrygia and Galatia. And when they came to the border of Mysia, they tried to enter Bithynia, but the <u>Spirit</u> of Jesus <u>would</u> <u>not</u> <u>permit</u> <u>them</u>...."
Acts 16:6–7 (BSB)

We see, by this verse, the Holy Spirit *prevented* Paul and those with him, from going to Asia. Also, when they tried to enter Bithynia, the Spirt would not permit them. Paul was *not* given the governmental mantle for both Asia and Bithynia, at that time. If this happened to Paul, what makes us think *we* can go to cities and regions without the Spirit giving us that mandate? Remember the seven sons of Sceva and those disastrous results, so do not take on ruling demons without a call to do so.

If we *are* called, make sure we stay within the sphere of authority God has given us, and don't take on more than what He has specifically given us to do. There is also danger in over–stepping the authority given to us. If we are called to a city, don't try to take on a region or nation; others will be given that assignment. They will be given the authority to accomplish what God has given *them* to do. If we take on more than we have been given divine authority for, the demonic realm also recognizes this and it makes us an open target. Yikes!

Staying in the sphere of authority we have been given comes with divine protection. This type of calling for city, regional, or national transformation is reserved for apostolic leaders who have been given that sphere of authority by God. This same protection is also given to those apostolic and prophetic leaders who are called to *assist* them in their assignment. Angels will also be assigned by the Lord, to help them in their regional work. Taking a region requires moving demonic structures out of the way, and the Lord gives strategies to those He *calls* for that assignment. He will show them in detail through visions, words of knowledge, and prophetic words, specifically what needs to be done for regional transformation.

Lord, I declare we will truly understand how to co-labor with angels and learn to stay within the authority we've been given, so that God would empower us to walk powerfully in the unique assignments He has for our life. In Jesus' name, Amen.

SECRET KINGDOM PRINCIPLES

Angels are ministering spirits sent to serve us.

Angels are ministers who bring the Word of God to pass.

We are given the power to restore *friendly relations* between God and man; and man with man.

Demonic rulers know and recognize those who have true authority *given* to them by God for a region, and those who don't.

Chapter 11

KEYS TO AN OPEN HEAVEN

"Give and it will be given to you. A good measure, pressed down, shaken together, and running over, will be poured into your lap. For with the measure you use, it will be measured to you."
Luke 6:38

Another secret and way to truly advance in the Kingdom of God is to walk in a spirit of Generosity.

Learn to walk in a spirit of generosity.

This was such a difficult lesson to learn, as I used to walk in a spirit of poverty. In my earlier walk with the Lord, I was anything but generous, as I lived in such fear there wasn't enough money for us to give because we needed it just to survive. Conversely, we may also have a lot of money and still walk in a spirit of poverty; for it is actually *fear of lack – the fear of never having enough.* It is an attitude and stronghold which prevents people from being able to be generous and must be dealt with.

A poverty spirit *always* walks in fear of lack.

Most of my Christian life I tithed, but God began to speak to me about being more generous in my giving. I remember telling the Lord I would be willing to give anything – except my diamond engagement ring. It was the most valuable, treasured thing I owned and had great sentimental value. However, it wasn't too long after that, the Lord asked me to do just that – give it away. What made His request even harder was that I didn't think I would be giving it into good soil. That ministry needed help, but I really didn't want to do it and really struggled within myself. In sheer obedience to God, I gave it into their ministry and it seemed as though I didn't' see any results from this offering. It wasn't until sometime later I realized by this one act of obedience, the spirit of poverty had been broken in my life and I had learned to become a generous giver.

I also learned God always blesses our obedience, even when we don't understand His reasons for something. We just need to trust Him because it's always for our ultimate good!

"You shall bring the first of the first fruits of your land, you shall bring into the house of the Lord your God."
Exodus 23:19 (KJB)

And also:

"And Abram gave him a <u>tenth</u> (the tithe) of everything."
Genesis 14:20

The Lord began to bring me to an understanding of the first fruits offering. Back in biblical days, they had crops and live-stock, which comprised *their* livelihood. In the present, it is a job that provides *our* livelihood. So they gave God the very first of the first fruits of their crops and livestock, which means they gave the Lord *His* tithe before anyone else received anything.

It is called a tithe which means: *'ten percent.'* There are a lot of Christians who give but a lot less than the ten percent tithe. There are also people who don't give consistently! Malachi 3:10–11 says to bring the *whole tithe* into the storehouse, so there may be food in God's house. God also said to test Him in this to see if He would not open the windows of heaven, and pour out so much blessing that we wouldn't have enough room to store it. He also promises He would keep pests from devour-ing our crops – our livelihood.

This was quite a promise from the Lord, that if I were to bring Him the *whole tithe* (ten percent), He would do all that for me. It sounded to me like the best plan I had heard, as no one could ever out give the Lord!

The Lord began speaking to me about tithing on our gross income rather than our net income. He showed me that if we tithed on our net, the government would be getting our *first of the first fruits* in the form of taxes, and we would actually be giving God ten percent of what *remained.* After understanding this truth, I obeyed and began to tithe on our gross income. *The first of the first fruits belong to the Lord!*

After doing this, we began to reap so much transformation in our lives, our family, marriage, and ministry. I attribute it all to obeying and believing the promise of blessings found in Malachi 3. We reap not only in our finances, but also in every area of our life. Malachi said to test Him, which I did and found this verse to be true.

God is a generous, sacrificial giver, and if we are to be transformed into His character and become like Him, we must learn to be a generous giver who gives joyfully without any strings attached. We should not look to man to be our source but to God, Who according to Psalm 50:10, owns all the cattle on a thousand hills. He has every resource in heaven reserved for those who tap into His principles and become, as it says in 2 Corinthians 9:7, cheerful givers.

We started by giving our tithe from the Old Testament, which is really the *minimum* we are to give. In the New Testament, which is a new and better covenant, there is *always more* – not less. I realized that ten percent was just the *minimum*, so we started sowing gifts above and beyond the tithe.

At the beginning they were small gifts, but as the Lord prospered us, our gifts became larger and larger. The Lord would tell us to whom and how much to give and we would obey whatever He told us to do. We didn't try to give to everyone and everybody, but followed the Holy Spirit's leading in where to give. My husband and I vowed to trust God to be our provider, and never looked to see if we could afford to obey him. God was always faithful to us!

"Now He, who supplies seed to the sower and bread for food will also supply and increase your store of seed and will enlarge the harvest of your righteousness. You will be enriched in every

way to be <u>generous</u> <u>on</u> <u>every</u> <u>occasion</u> and your giving
through us will produce thanksgiving to God."
2 Corinthians 9:10

God supplies seed (finances) to the sower, which means in order to receive seed from His hand, we *first* need to become a sower (giver). It also tells us, for those who sow, He will increase our store of seed and enlarge our harvest. This way, we can be generous on every occasion because we will have more money than we need and resources in our storehouse to give with.

In our years of giving, we have seen supernatural and miraculous provision by His hand. I want to share *one* example of how He has fulfilled this promise. He asked us to give two very large gifts and a small one at the same time. At this point in our Christian walk, we never questioned God in our giving. One of the larger gifts was to someone who was praying for resources they needed. Not only did they pray for the financial need to be met, but also asked the Lord to speak to someone they had blessed to provide it. It was an honor to be able to be used to financially bless them, as they have been a huge blessing to us.

Another gift was sowed to someone who needed to make a decision. It was an answer to her prayer, "Lord, if you really want me to do this, then give me the amount I need to confirm this is Your will." The Lord instructed me to tell her the Lord said, this was her confirmation. It was the exact amount she asked God for!

God supplies to those who have needs and He meets them by using those who have learned to become generous givers. It is so fulfilling and gives us great joy to be able to be the instrument of answered prayer. We are in no way financially well–

off–yet, but God knows that whatever we have, we make available to Him. It's the *only* way for us to live!

This is just one testimony of the miraculous provisions the Lord has used us for. That next month, we received an unexpected letter in the mail. The letter told us we had stocks that were valued at double the amount we gave and they wanted to send us the monetary value of them. We didn't know we owned those stocks. A miracle? The Lord brought back to us double what He asked us to send. The bottom line is, we were blessed in being a blessing to others. We really do reap what we sow! We didn't give to get, and certainly didn't expect to be blessed that way, as we just obey God and He does what He does so well.

I could give so many examples of His miraculous provisions, for God always gives more seed to the sower. Let's remember this secret:

God promises to give us more seed if we are a sower.

Lately, we have been reaping from other people, which is new for us, as we have always been the sowers. Someone gave me a beautiful ring which they said the Lord told them to give. This ring actually fulfilled a promise the Lord gave me a few years before, which opened the door to more authority and power to Kingdom government in my life. He *also* showed me this ring was given by *His* hand to replace that engagement ring I sowed over ten years before. This *new* ring was someone's garnet wedding band. I realized I had come full circle from that day, so many years ago, when I was asked to sow my engagement ring. God revealed to me that with this ring gift, I moved from being engaged to a wedding with Him. I was so amazed at what He said, as God is so good!

"Give, and it will be given to you. They will pour into your lap a good measure – pressed down, shaken together, and running over. For by your standard of measure it will be measured to you in return."
Luke 6:38

**By the standard of measure we give to other people,
God will measure that back to us in return.**

If we learn to be generous givers, we are promised by the Lord to receive pressed down, shaken together, and running over. I know *firsthand* this verse is so true

In today's church, it's understood and accepted, that the pastor receives a salary from the church which comes from the tithes of those who attend. But Paul, in Philippians 4:15, was an itinerant traveling minister. He told us no other church supported him through giving at that time, except the Philippian church. I wonder what had happened to the rest of those churches and why they didn't support him?

Paul has a *lot* to say about giving to ministers; possibly because the Philippian church was the only one who gave.

"For it is written in the Law of Moses: 'Do not muzzle an ox while it is treading out the grain.' Is it about oxen that God is concerned? Surely he says this for us, doesn't he? Yes, this was written for us. If we have sown spiritual seed among you, is it

*too much if we reap a material harvest from you? In the same
way, the Lord has commanded that those who preach the
gospel should receive their living from the gospel."*
I Corinthians 9:9–14

**God has commanded that those who minister the gospel
should receive their living from the gospel.**

Those in ministry were not only to receive their living from
the Gospel, in order to have their financial needs met, but it
says the *Lord commanded* it. It also says, if they sow spiritual
seed to others, they should reap a material harvest from them.

How did we miss that?

Some years ago, we went back up north where I received an
extensive three–hour inner healing session from two seasoned
ministers; one of which was a good friend. I didn't sow into
their ministry at that time because I didn't have the understanding that I should. This was the result of wrong thinking
and teaching about this. So, the following year, because I had
come into a *new* understanding of the importance to giving in
this type of ministry, the Lord had me sow a generous gift to
my friend to share with the other minister.

After receiving a prophetic word, the Lord instructed me to
leave my full–time career to go into full–time ministry. I had
come to this new understanding after starting my own ministry and needing to depend on the Lord for personal provision
from the ministry. Those who had poured into me for my inner
healing were worthy of my sowing into them for helping me

get healed. I came to understand that I needed to *honor* them with my *gift*, as they were used to transform my life and had no source of income for their gas, rent, food, and all other expenses needed for them to be free to minister to everyone. It was also *God's command*, according to verse 14 above!

Church, we really need to grab hold of a radical understanding on this subject and begin to be more generous to those who live by the Gospel and minister to us.

"For scripture says, 'Do not muzzle an ox while it is treading out the grain,' and 'The worker deserves his wages.'"
I Timothy 5:18

Paul needed support and so did *Jesus,* along with the apostles, as they traveled around ministering. The financial resources needed to come in as *gifts* so they had food, shelter, clothing, and everything else they needed to minister to the masses in the towns and cities they traveled to. During the New Testament time, the tithe went to the local synagogue.

"So I thought it necessary to urge the brothers to visit you in advance and finish the arrangements for the generous gift you promised. Then it will be ready as a generous gift, not as one grudgingly given."
2 Corinthians 9:5

Paul sent someone to gather the monetary gifts promised, exhorted them to be ready with a generous gift, and to not give grudgingly. God said, in 2 Corinthians 9:6, if we sow sparingly, we will reap sparingly, and in verse 5, that He loves a cheerful giver. Wow, when we give generously to others, God loves it! Don't we want to do the things God loves? If we read through the New Testament, it has an awful lot to say about support, money, generosity, and supporting those who minister to us.

I know so many Christians who are so uncomfortable hearing about tithing and giving, but they are truly missing out on the *greatest blessings* from heaven by withholding their giving. There is also a wrong teaching and attitude I've heard, which says people should minister for free and not receive anything for it. The truth is, there *is no charge* for ministering, but *Jesus* and the *apostles* received financial gifts from those they ministered to. My question is this – how did they pay for the places they stayed, the food they needed, the care of their families as they traveled, and the money needed to travel to places to minister?

The scriptures I shared should cause us to rethink what our attitudes should be. *We just don't understand, as we honor God with our finances, it means we honor those who minister to us.* Our money can't go to God directly, but can and should go to those whom the Word specifies it should. Those who live by the Gospel need to make their living that way, as *God commands it.*

I have been a tither and generous giver for a very long time. I've given to speakers who came to our church, and now, becoming generous to those who are not leaders of a church that have salaries, but who minister to me. Before, I took for granted those who took time to pour into my life, as I didn't have the proper understanding I needed to sow financially into them. Now, I know! We are called to honor those who minister amongst us, and one of the ways we do that is to help support them; honor is an action, as honor always looks like something!

It's truly a matter of honoring them and their time as they

pour themselves out to minister to others. I aspire to always be growing and increasing in my revelation and understanding of the Word of God and how to apply it to life's situations. I want to continue to be a generous sower and reap generously, especially since I now understand, being in full–time ministry. This is the *promise* for generosity found in the New Testament.

> *"And God is able to bless you abundantly so that in all things at all times, having all you need, you will abound in every good work."*
> 2 Corinthians 9:8

Begin to give generously to all who minister to us, to those who have needs; and finally, bring the whole tithe into the storehouse.

When starting to become a giver, my husband was the only one working. We had four children, and very little money. Remember the widow who gave everything she had, when she gave her mite? The Lord trained me to begin giving what I had, even though it didn't seem like much. As we are faithful with a little, the Lord trusts us and gives us more. The truth of the matter is, if we haven't learned to give when we have a little money, we *won't* give when we have more. The Word is pretty clear in Luke:

> *"He who is faithful in a very little thing is faithful also in much; and he who is unrighteous in a very little thing is unrighteous also in much. Therefore, if you have not been faithful in the use of unrighteous wealth, who will entrust the true riches to you? And if you have not been faithful in the use of that which is*

another's, who will give you that which is your own?"
Luke 16:10–12 (NASB)

This verse says, if we have not been faithful in the use of that which is another's, who will give us that which is our own? To paraphrase this: If we have not been faithful with the money which is another's (God's), then God won't give us more (our own). You see, God has *commanded* us to both *tithe* and *give* generously, so that money actually *belongs* to Him. Ouch, if we don't look at it from His perspective.

If we have not been generous when we have a little money, we won't be generous when we have more!

People say, "I will give when I have more money to give," but we can see from the verses in Luke 16, this isn't true. My life would have been so different had I not learned to be generous, beginning with the tithe, which is the minimum, and had not grown into gifts and offerings. Proverbs 13:22 says, the sinner's wealth is stored up for the righteous. I want to be righteous, as it pertains to generosity; and I'm standing in faith for the resources to give and to receive for every good work.

Lord, I declare those who are reading this chapter are becoming the most generous people who have an abundance of resources for the good works the Lord gives them to do, and are a blessing to others with their resources. I am declaring this new revelation will break the poverty mentality and bring a paradigm shift to those who are reading this chapter. That they will see the truth about tithing, giving, and how it will transform their lives! I also declare the Lord will give them even more seed, as they become very generous sowers. In Jesus' name, Amen.

SECRET KINGDOM PRINCIPLES

Learn to walk in a spirit of generosity.

A poverty spirit *always* walks in fear of Lack.

God promises to give us more seed if we are a sower.

By the standard of measure we give to other people,
God will measure that back to us in return.

God has commanded that those who minister the gospel
should receive their living from the gospel.

Begin to give generously to all who minister to us, to
those who have needs; and finally, bring the whole
tithe into the storehouse.

If we have not been generous when we have a little money,
we won't be generous when we have more!

Daniel 2:22 He reveals the deep and secret things…

WILL WE PAY THE PRICE?

"For whoever wants to save their life will lose it, but whoever loses their life for Me will find it."
Matthew 16:25

According to Isaiah 53:5, by Jesus' wounds we are healed, so we have been given the promise to be healed and set free. SOZO, the word used for salvation, also means nothing broken and nothing missing – that means body, soul, and spirit!

I am excited to see what God has in store for the Church in this reformation season we find ourselves in. Imagine a church that is so healed – body, soul, and spirit – and walks the earth as Jesus did in absolute, unconditional love with signs and wonders following them everywhere they go!

We want to see the Church begin to operate from heaven to earth, once again establishing the five–fold divine order set forth in the Word of God. The Church would become a place where multitudes run to, in contrast to what the world has to offer. This will be a church filled with the glory of God radiating from the Bride without spot or blemish; this is reformation at its highest level!

To be a reformer, we will be used to restore God's original design set forth in His Word.

I've shared my journey, up to this point in my life and know there are so many *new* secrets to be revealed in this next season; to go even deeper and higher in the Kingdom of God. But, I also know that following the principles shared in this book will take us into greater authority being released in our life.

We can't camp on the scriptures we like, ones that are fun and easy to follow, as Jesus learned obedience by the things He suffered. He gave us this example in sacrificing all He had in heaven to die for our sins. He not only gave us an example to follow but also gave us the power to be transformed into His image. There is always a great price that comes with being promoted by the hand of God. Jesus was our example and paid the ultimate price in giving His life for us!

Those who are willing to sacrifice everything in order to obey *all* His commands, and not just the *easy* ones, are those whom the Spirit is seeking for this new season of the Church. These will hear what the Spirit is saying, and will be the ones who transition away from the traditions of men to return to God's original design found in His Word. It is those who will search the Word of God to see if what is actually taught by men is *truly* what the Lord is saying.

"Now the Bereans were more noble-minded than the Thessalonians, for they received the message with great eagerness and examined the Scriptures every

day to see if these teachings were true."
Acts 17:11 (BSB)

**The Bereans examined the Scriptures to see if what
was taught was the truth, as we also should.**

We see that the Bereans were more noble–minded and received the apostles' teachings with great eagerness. Yet, at the same time, they were *examining* the Scriptures for themselves to see if what they taught was true. We need to become more like a Berean as we hear *our* teachers tell us what the Word of God says. We need to examine the Word for ourselves, and also depend on the Holy Spirit, to see if what we're hearing taught from others, is the truth!

I came to the Lord well over forty years ago and was such an emotional mess. I know that without Jesus in my life, I couldn't even imagine what my life and family would have been like. I had no love to offer anyone, until He came and loved me enough to transform my life and put me in His Kingdom. He removed all the fear, self–hatred, rejection, insecurity, rebellion, control, anger, so much more, and replaced it with the love of God and His love for people.

He truly does take our greatest weaknesses and turns them into our greatest strengths! I was in need of such transformation and now transformation is the passion of my heart and life. That weakness has become my life's work, my passion, and what I live for: to see transformation of lives, regions, nations, as well as in the Church.

Heaven is searching for those who are hungry for
the secrets of the Kingdom and willing to
give their *all* to walk in them!

I encourage us to press into the Kingdom of God like never
before, and allow His Word to transform us. Don't settle for
merely the Gifts of the Spirit, but press in to obtain the Fruit of
the Spirit; until we walk in *all* of them and they are increasing
in our life.

"But the fruit of the Spirit is love, joy, peace, patience, kindness,
goodness, faithfulness. But the greatest of these is love,
for love never fails."
Galatians 5:22

Lastly, may our *caves* lead us to the *secrets* of the Kingdom
being released in our life, to launch us to new heights and
depths, but also deeper into our divine destiny!

My prayer for us, is for Kingdom secrets to be revealed, so we
may be transformed and mature enough to walk in those great
assignments the Lord has written in our book!

Lord, I declare those who read this book will press in for the
secret Kingdom principles to enter deeper into the Kingdom of
God. They will rejoice in giving their entire life in submission
to living out the Word of God, and be willing to pay any price
needed! I declare they will teach others how to live life excited
and will increase in the truth contained in the living Word that
transforms lives. I am also declaring, those who find Your se-

crets will be released into the great destinies You have for them, to change atmospheres and transform lives, cities, regions, and nations. Lastly, that they will become loving reformers in this new season of the Ecclesia. In Jesus' name, Amen!

SECRET KINGDOM PRINCIPLES

To be a reformer, we will be used to restore God's original design set forth in His Word.

The Bereans examined the Scriptures to see if what was taught was the truth, as we also should.

Heaven is searching for those who are hungry for the secrets of the Kingdom and willing to give their *all* to walk in them!

Note: If you would like a printed copy of *ALL* the Secret Kingdom Principles listed in the book, please go to the bottom of the book page on our website for a free download:

www.ReformationCenter.net/secrets–revealed

MEET THE AUTHOR

As Senior Leader and founder of Reformation Center, whose vision is "Restoring God's Original Design," Linda Santangelo's desire is to see lives and regions walking out the love of the father in every realm they are called to and to see them being released into their destiny.

She is a passionate speaker, ordained minister, and apostolic teacher whose life's pursuit is to see lives transformed. Linda is passionate to see reformation come to individuals, churches and regions, to see them released into the authority of the Kingdom and supernatural realms.

She has a heart to see the five–fold ministry restored to the Church in order to reestablish divine order in the Kingdom of God from heaven to earth.

She has authored these books: *Secrets Revealed –A Journey into Kingdom Principles, Designed for Destiny*, and the *Designed for Destiny – Guide* workbook.

Linda lives in Florida with her husband Vinnie, and has four children and two grandchildren.

DESIGNED FOR DESTINY

We have a destiny to fulfill during our time on earth because we have all been *Designed for Destiny*. So many of us fall short of achieving all we desire and have no idea what God has predestined us to do. Even if we do understand we have a destiny, we may not understand that we could be set free from the obstacles that are standing in the way.

There is a quickening of great desire arising in the Body of Christ to know and understand why we are living so far below the call of God in our life. We are also beginning to suspect that God has more in store for us than what we have seen evidenced. Hope is springing up and we are looking for answers to the cry of our heart.

Do you want to be set free from the hindrances and obstacles in the path of your destiny?

If so, *Designed for Destiny* answers many questions and will help remove many obstacles to seeing and fulfilling that great plan God has for us!

You may order this book on our website or on Amazon:

www.ReformationCenter.net/designed–for–destiny

We have also written a *Designed for Destiny – Guide,* as a companion workbook to *Designed for Destiny*, to greatly enhance and reinforce what we are learning about the healing process in our lives. This *Guide* may be used individually or in small groups.

 The *Designed for Destiny – Guide* is available to order on our web-site's book page, or on Amazon.

www.ReformationCenter.net/designed–for–destiny

Reformation Center – "Restoring God's Original Design"

Bradenton, Florida

If you are interested in having Linda speak at your church or group, host a conference, or to let us know how reading *Secrets Revealed* has transformed your life, please email us at:

info@ReformationCenter.org

Website: www.ReformationCenter.org

www.LindaSantangelo.com

Follow us on Facebook and YouTube:

www.facebook.com/linsantangelo (public page)

www.facebook.com/SecretsRevealedBook/

www.facebookcom/DesignedForDestinyBook/

www.youtube.com/user/linsantangelo

Daniel 2:22 He reveals the deep and secret things...

www.ingramcontent.com/pod-product-compliance
Lightning Source LLC
LaVergne TN
LVHW051520080426
835509LV00017B/2128